"There may be no more pressing matter for the emerging world of 21st-century capitalism than the question of addiction. Up until now, the current array of theoretical formulations for addiction as a concept and social set of practices, both remediative and explanatory, have been of limited utility. This volume offers an innovative and convincing intervention into how we might think of addiction as an integral aspect of contemporary capitalist logic and as a way of understanding emerging modes of alternative engagements that may offer new worlds and new peoples. Utilizing Deleuzo-Guattarian schizoanalytics the book offers both overdue new methodological tactics of inquiry as well as introducing addiction as a social configuration rather than an individual pathology. The proposals for new forms of sociality and subjectivity offer life affirming alternatives to the death drive of late stage capitalism."

— **Hans Skott-Myhre,** *Professor of Human Services, Kennesaw State University, USA*

INTERNET ADDICTION

This essential book questions the psychological construct of Internet Addiction by contextualizing it within the digital technological era. It proposes critical psychology that investigates user subjectivity as a function of capitalism and imperialism, arguing against punitive models of digital excesses and critiquing the political economy of the Internet affecting all users.

Friedman explores the limitations of individual-centered remediations exemplified in the psychology of Internet Addiction. Furthermore, Friedman outlines the self-creative actions of social media users and the data processing that exploits them to urge psychologists to politicize rather than pathologize the effects of excessive net use. The book develops a notion of capitalist imperialism of the social web and studies this using the radical methods of philosopher Gilles Deleuze, and psychoanalyst Félix Guattari.

By synthesizing perspectives on digital life from sociology, economics, digital media theory, and technology studies for psychologists, this book will be of interest to academics and students in these areas, as well as psychologists and counselors interested in addressing Internet Addiction as a collective, societal ill.

Emaline Friedman, Ph.D., is an independent scholar and psychoanalytic theorist. Her research interests cover all forms of digital control and exploitation: data capitalism, platform labor, AI-enabled bigotry, and software cultures. She works on distributed ledger technologies to steer networked social organization toward human solidarity initiatives, environmental regeneration, and other forms of commoning.

Concepts for Critical Psychology: Disciplinary Boundaries Re-thought

Series editor: Ian Parker

Developments inside psychology that question the history of the discipline and the way it functions in society have led many psychologists to look outside the discipline for new ideas. This series draws on cutting edge critiques from just outside psychology in order to complement and question critical arguments emerging inside. The authors provide new perspectives on subjectivity from disciplinary debates and cultural phenomena adjacent to traditional studies of the individual.

The books in the series are useful for advanced level undergraduate and postgraduate students, researchers and lecturers in psychology and other related disciplines such as cultural studies, geography, literary theory, philosophy, psychotherapy, social work and sociology

Deleuze and Psychology
Philosophical Provocations to Psychological Practices
Maria Nichterlein & John R. Morss

Rethinking Education through Critical Psychology
Cooperative schools, Social Justice and Voice
Gail Davidge

Developing Minds
Psychology, Neoliberalism and Power
Elise Klein

Marxism and Psychoanalysis
In or Against Psychology?
David Pavón-Cuéllar

Decentering Subjectivity in Everyday Eating and Drinking
Digesting Reality
Ali Lara

Internet Addiction
A Critical Psychology of Users
Emaline Friedman

For more information about this series, please visit: https://www.routledge.com/Concepts-for-Critical-Psychology/book-series/CONCEPTSCRIT

INTERNET ADDICTION

A Critical Psychology of Users

Emaline Friedman

Routledge
Taylor & Francis Group

LONDON AND NEW YORK

First published 2021
by Routledge
2 Park Square, Milton Park, Abingdon, Oxon OX14 4RN

and by Routledge
605 Third Avenue, New York, NY 10017

Routledge is an imprint of the Taylor & Francis Group, an informa business

British Library Cataloguing-in-Publication Data
A catalog record for this book is available from the British Library

Library of Congress Cataloging-in-Publication Data
A catalog record has been requested for this book

ISBN 13: 978-0-367-17291-6 (hbk)
ISBN 13: 978-0-367-17295-4 (pbk)

Typeset in Bembo
by MPS Limited, Dehradun

CONTENTS

FOREWORD

This book enables critique and action, and that means the author would most probably be labeled an "enabler" in the pop-addiction literature that thinks it knows what things we should get hooked on and what we should not. Pop-addiction literature, whether through twelve steps or more subtle cues about preferred pathways out of self-harm and to redemption, feeds and is fed by the discipline of psychology. Psychology itself is the explicit or implicit source-point for many of the competing models of addiction that ostensibly explain why people become attached to certain practices. Still, it rarely reflects on the underlying assumptions about the nature of human subjectivity that so-often disable users while declaring that it only intends to help them find the right path. We urgently need to step away from these assumptions, and this book shows that conceptual innovations developed by Gilles Deleuze and Félix Guattari can help us do that. Their work will lead us somewhere else entirely, and the journey is more important than the destination. In place of the promise of a quick fix that will serve to unhook us from our addiction to the circular repetitive little fixes of much internet activity is a "critical psychology of users."

Are we not all users of psychology? Is not the deepest cultural-historical conceptual pit today that of psychology itself, the discipline that pretends to offer solutions to our ills while encouraging us to dig ourselves deeper into it, into the pit itself? Is not the most radical challenge Deleuze and Guattari pose not to this or that addiction, in this case "Internet Addiction," but to the network of theories and practices that turn our experience of use and misuse into something psychological, into something inside of us instead of inhering within the architecture of the web? The discipline of psychology is an intimate part of that web of knowledge and interaction, its helpmeet, and then its misleading diagnostician. Emaline Friedman shows us how and why psychology must be refused if we are to get anywhere other than back into the pit.

"Addiction," we are told time and again, glues us to our objects of desire, as if those objects are already commonsensical delimited things and as if there was a healthy and morally worthy way of seeking out those things, obtaining them and owning them. This book delves deeper, and not into the psychology of the "user," to lay bare the way that this process of turning a process of human activity into "things" is at one with the "thingification" or "reification" that contemporary capitalism needs – is addicted to, we might say – as the bedrock of its ideological operations. Psychology is down there in the depths of all this, but it is capitalism that is the pits. We need to forge a quite different critical psychology of users that can break from the toxic relation to things that enables addiction as such to appear on the horizon of human subjectivity. That means that a book like *Internet Addiction* must work inside the terrain of the concept "addiction" in order to show how it marks out a particular kind of territory. In the alternative discourse Deleuze and Guattari give us, we "deterritorialize" addiction, breaking it open, working "outwith" it. Then new horizons appear for subjectivity that this book charts with optimism and conceptual rigor.

Ian Parker,
University of Manchester

1
INTRODUCTION

Introduction

When I first began thinking about addiction, I was not thinking about addiction to the Internet. I became involved in twelve-step programs by my addict father's belief that I should use it to cure a sudden and comparatively short-lived bout of anorexia by going through the program. He fashioned me as addicted to deprivation, a formulation that gripped me. Especially given its paradoxical quality, I found this mode of treatment too compelling not to test out. What I found was not extraordinary – a room of the unfortunate, not unlike the televised representations one sees in passing. Stories are shared, donations are made, and the refrain persists: "Hi, I'm whoever, and I'm an alcoholic." This facet gripped me, too. How is it that admission, or submission (as it appeared to me at the time), holds the key to greater agency?

I type "agency" pointedly, with a touch of mockery. One must not be fooled into believing that this confers a greater sense of control (self- or otherwise). It is precisely giving up control, handing it over to one's "higher power" that enables one to get a handle on the so-called disease of addiction. On the one hand, there would seem to be a sort of magic of language at play: a performative insistence, like a ritual or rite, which enacts a critical reflexive function sufficient for change. On the other, there is a community of addicts who use this term as a social currency that defines inclusion and belonging, heralding exactly those things sought by the addict – those things for which drugs and alcohol, psychological thinkers will tell us, are impoverished substitutions. In twelve-step meetings, one sees the dynamics of power via subjection play out, not in any theater of social or political power, but entirely within the locus of the self. Gregory Bateson (2000) characterized this fix long ago as changing the structure of pride endemic to addicts. Where alcoholism is placed outside the self, "I can resist drinking," the twelve-step program relocates alcoholism *within* the self. It is a solution offered along the lines of imaginary identification with a disease entity that preys on this self. This identification has the dual function of forming individuals, modeled on Western liberal political subjects of internality, and then directing their behavior. In the case of twelve-step programs, the behavior is directed away from the drug-object, whatever it may be.

Today one can play out the role of the mental health professional by characterizing any experience of excess or dependency as an addiction. My abbreviated story above, along with the thirty-six adaptations of the steps for different drugs indexed by Wikipedia, testify to this normative understanding. It seems possible to offer up any human phenomenon to the implicitly psychological-institutional mode of social life. In the case of addiction, addicts are often sold another fix, like a retreat, mindfulness training, hypnosis, or Methadone (as in treatment for addiction to heroin). Community-run twelve-step groups stand as a rare, grassroots exception, though their structure and logic are commonly layered with other more individually targeted components of treatment by psy-professionals.

Psychology was formulated to carry out extremely specific policing functions in the Anglophone world, with a model of mental health that has since also spread its style of understanding human beings to the global South. While diagnoses and their logic have permeated the globe, they have again plunged deeper into the body, with a swelling scope of influence over increased facets of human life. For example, in *Glow Kids* (2017), Dr. Nicholas Kardaras, Harvard psychologist and CEO of "Maui Recovery" in Hawaii, looks at how "age-inappropriate screen tech" is ravaging an entire "iGen" – the first generation to spend their entire adolescence with smartphones. Neuroscientific discourses typically have the last word on "addiction creep," when images of the brain show that glowing screens are as stimulating and "dopaminergic" (dopamine activating) to the brain's pleasure centers as sex or drugs more widely acknowledged to be addictive. Most shocking of all, recent brain imaging studies conclusively show that excessive screen exposure can neurologically damage a young person's developing brain in the same way that cocaine addiction can.

Whether attributed from outside or incorporated intentionally by the subject of psychological diagnoses, the diagnostic label acts as a social currency that affords access to these treatment options. This is a double-edged sword when one considers the barrage of stigmatizing cultural associations it also carries from centuries of staunch disciplining of drug users by various government agencies. Many critically-minded characterizations of the current explosion of addiction pathologies, like Internet and Social Media Addiction, highlight how these discourses produced top-down restraints on life, calling them "civilizing technolog[ies]" (Vrecko, 2010), or "medicalization[s] of deviance" (Schneider, 1978). Such characterizations unsettle and de-naturalize addiction pathologies through genealogical accounts of its production through the intersections of science, psychology, and public policy (see also Christensen, 2015). In America, drug-taking has been intermittently seen as a form of protest, rebellion, artistry, sociality, criminality, illness, and experimentation. Foucault (1965), among many others (see Levine, 1978), links the late-19th century medico-juridical discourse of "toxicomania" to the mania operating in the hierarchizing science of types that attempted to order the elements of the world following their functions (rather than their forms). The taxonomic impulse that characterized and formed the human and biological scientific discourses created the conditions for the psychopathological entity "addiction" to emerge alongside medical, judicial, and social institutions (i.e., welfare).

Recently the World Health Organization added digital gaming disorder to the 11th revision of the ICD (Gaebel et al., 2017) and the APA recategorizing non-substance related behaviors, like internet gambling, together with substance-use disorders in the DSM (Potenza, 2014). It is not only Psychology that responds to the large-scale social changes wrought by ubiquitous digital communication. Owing, perhaps, to the massively widespread phenomenon that is the Internet, the barrage of voices outside of psychology concerned with excessive use of the Internet, particularly social media, hearken back to this pre-psy-industrial history, even as it imports its concepts. News outlets like CBS and NBC foment this discourse, citing anecdotal self-reports, buffeted by scant, early-stage neurological research, to proclaim that users are no match for the tantalizing pleasures of the net-connected screen that hijacks users' brains. Supporting their outcry with analogical reasoning, psychological experiments point to the similarity between the brains of World of Warcraft addicts, slot machine players, and heroin addicts as they are preparing to play or to inject.

In early 2018 at the World Economic Forum in Davos, George Soros joined the ranks of high-profile businessmen who criticized the harmful effects of major Internet platforms (Solon, 2018). There, even early investors of Facebook, the chunk of the Net this text focuses on, wondered what the platform does to "our children's brains," flirting with the notion that its growth could be considered a threat to public health (McNamee, 2017).

The problem of screen time even made it onto the democratic debate stage in the early days of 2020 United States presidential campaigning. Screen time is easily politicized in its linkage to fear of a nonhuman, "mechanistic" creep, portrayed in movies like *Terminator* (Daly et al., 1984) and *I, Robot* (Baron et al., 2004). These movies typically end with robots and intelligent machines, forming a new sort of violent or hyper-conscious revolution capable of taking over or overthrowing human domination of the natural world. Such fear makes an excellent campaign platform in a cultural climate where managerial fantasies of humans' replacement by fully obedient, laboring machines are repeatedly presented as a new horizon of capitalism.

Responses from the tech sector include suggestions by other executives that its major platforms be regulated just like cigarette companies. Note that these responses take addictiveness and the addiction paradigm for granted (Hern, 2018). And the companies have responded with suites of tools like the Time Well Spent initiative, meant to help individuals monitor their social media use. Just like methadone treatments for heroin, the irony is that a new net-connected application trains you away from the old one. The brain disease model of addiction finds a correlate in the tracking and monitoring functions of such apps, where the whole user (rather than the brain taken in isolation) must be notified, nudged, and discouraged from engaging with the mobile phone or social platform - once they appease the tracking app, that is. Public sector responses have considered measures like the "Social Media Addiction Reduction Technology Act" (or the SMART Act, for short). Recall, again, that this pathological entity is not recognized by Psychology's DSM, but easily gains recognition before the United States Congress. In this act, Congress finds that the business model of many social media companies is to capture as much of their user's attention as possible – a goal that exploits the brain physiology and human psychological vulnerabilities of users by design. These responses have created even more radical calls for closing Pandora's box. Social media, some say, should simply not exist at all.

Even outside of the psy-institutions, concern about screen time, social media addiction, and theft of the user's free choice are voiced from the outside looking in, even as the high-powered individuals in the technology and public sectors are undoubtedly users themselves. The excessive use of anything socially considered to be a "drug," however well-meaning, subjects it to the question of management and administration of a subject of pathological enjoyment. It is as if a whole chorus of concern chimes in, joining psychology's task through their own means. In the case of the Internet, it would seem that psychologists, care workers, lifestyle coaches, health gurus, politicians, business executives, the World Health Organization, Alcoholics

Anonymous fanatics, or really any player interested in human well-being might be motivated to (and likely equally unsuccessful at) intervening in this presumed problem of consumption.

In its evocative capacity, scholars have even turned to Internet Addiction to understand how the average citizen thinks about the Internet as a threat to their family, their peace of mind, and their way of life (Manjikian, 2016). Thus, as an object of discourse, Internet Addiction explores how we think about the function of the net and its impact on society at large. Likewise, this book seeks a critical understanding of excessive activity on the Internet, surveying scholarly expressions of concern about the automation of already-precarious jobs, obsolescence of other skills and abilities through the digitization of all parts of life, algorithms increasingly taking control of users' experience of the world, and the general disorientation of radical social change owing to digitalism. These are some of the fear-based pathos that shrouds our orientation to the realities of what *is in fact emerging* on the Internet.

If psychologists and others are pointing out a psychical pandemic of sorts, might we need something more than a diagnostic label tethered to individual subjects? As it stands, the discourse of neuroscience and accompanying images of the brain are wielded in order to locate addiction squarely within the heads of individual persons. Such delimited stigma is a manifestation of psychological institutions' maintenance of the myth of the "individual," on whom it relies to peddle its services. I begin with a brief look at how addictive disorders in general and Internet Addiction in particular are deployed within psychology as a diagnostic category. Internet Addiction concerns a problem of excess enjoyment related to the use of the Internet, as identified in psychological research and beyond. Yet, this grafting onto the Internet the diagnostic markers of addiction is a highly problematic overgeneralization of the addiction category, which itself mirrors the ballooning of the psychological industries and their simple, profit-driven templates for addressing a whole range of postmodern complaints and ascriptions of abnormality.

Given the meeting of addiction discourses and mounting awareness of the social changes wrought from the Internet, the voices of concern about Internet Addiction extend far beyond the grips of psychology. The transdisciplinary and even extra-academic imperative of this book comes from the object of study; neither the "addictification of society" (Loose, 2015) nor its digitization, pay much attention to the siloing of knowledge production as a form of violence against thought. Against the ever-expanding umbrella of addiction labeling, I argue that it is not habit *per se* that is problematic. In fact, philosopher Gilles Deleuze (1994) asserts that habit is the foundation from which all other psychic phenomena derive. Instead, I address a crucial paradox of Internet Addiction related to the historical usage of the signifier "addiction" and the recent, total shift it has undergone. Where addictions have generally called out an "anti-social" form of enjoyment, Internet Addiction is precisely a form of enjoyment *too* enraptured in *the dominant mode of sociality of the global society which it creates.* The current construction of Internet Addiction, however inadvertently, undercuts the reality, the social necessity, of participating in a globally connected world. It stigmatizes such dependence which, contrary to other "addictions," is based in human interdependence.

This is a form of *technofetishism* to which psychology falls prey – the fallacy of objectifying the human relations that make up the Internet. The word used by theorists to describe the transformation of a social process into a thing is "reification" – ("thing-ification") (Lukács & Livingstone, 2013). Reified as an object of addiction, the Internet's specific qualities are never determined. In this key, *the* software, *the* algorithm, and *the* platform appear as supernatural forces for users and mental health professionals alike, who, generally speaking, prefer not to know what – or whose gaze – is under the hood. The construction of the Internet as a drug, therefore, is not only erroneous but threatens to sharply limit psychologists' understanding of the Internet and its often-liberating affordances (especially for minoritarian social groups). The Internet here is a means of connection between actual people, which means its stigmatization pits the psychological individual against a collective of users. Moreover, with the Internet as the differentiated cultural milieu of global capitalism, psychology's characterization of Internet Addicts as passive victims swept up in its clutches is a little-acknowledged cultural insensitivity, ignoring the active participation of users that gives the social web its value. The weight of this insensitivity falls disproportionately on those who grew up online – "digital natives."

The piece then moves to an introduction of schizoanalysis, emphasizing a methodology particular to Deleuze and Guattari's Marxian politics that I argue is especially useful in dealing with digital technologies and the society to which they increasingly refer. While schizoanalysis is a radically flexible methodology, in the context of this piece, it produces a selective mapping of the digital social body to elucidate a schematic understanding of the meaning of addiction to the Internet according to the social stratifications that it creates and the means by which they are created. Through a deep dive into social media companies, infrastructure, and assets, including users, we confront digital capitalism, its apparatuses of capture, and its methods of control in their present forms. This method, schizoanalysis, suggests that universal history is an affordance of the capitalist social system that the Internet (as we know it in its current iteration) creates and recreates continuously. This method also posits the requisite philosophical, and psychoanalytical principles through which the promotion of existential values and a politics of desire might proceed. A politics of desire is, firstly, able to address the paradox of Internet Addiction noted above, and secondly, apt for addressing the problematization of desire and assessing its material effects – *what it produces, how, and to whose benefit and detriment.*

Going back to the fix offered by twelve-step groups: In the array of individualizing treatments offered by mental health professionals, treatment-by-community is a radical idea not to be taken for granted. The curiosity of Internet Addiction is that the very place that "community" ostensibly lives today is "within" the drug, as it were – the form that community takes in contemporary capitalism. A community of Internet users is just that: using together in the place they *have to be together* based on the capitalist imperialism of the digital world, furthered and assuaged through digital technological means. Users have to be together in the double sense that the Internet is commonly understood as a cultural affordance that enables new forms of sociality and in the sense of a migration beneficial for the processes of global capitalism. Having an online presence is increasingly required for interaction with migrated and new social institutions, like schools, state entities, banks, and businesses. The grip of capitalism's psychical and physical imperialism is therefore displaced onto the compelling drug-object and *its* sway over the unwitting (or ambivalent) psychologized subject of free will.

More and more of us *have to* be online, and migrant and nomadic users internalize bits and pieces of identities through practices of commercially bloated self-representation. The early days of the Internet cultivated a spirit of newfound freedom. Now, Internet-as-an-addiction directly contrasts any characterization of it (e.g. by social media companies) as a place of community. Even if one concedes that the Internet has drug-like properties, treating this problem individually and attempting to eliminate or moderate its use would still have the untenable consequence of extreme social exclusion for those so designated. The network structure of the organization that pervades trade, finance, business, and work rely on digitally mediated communication across long distances, use of complex computational instruments for processing massive quantities of data, and an eschewal of dominant frameworks of time or space in favor of labor that spreads across all other areas of life (Stalder, 2006). This networked style of connection also assumes a sort of proximity-of- everything that issues from the reach of market valorization into all areas of life and the mechanisms of surveillance and control by which such reach is accomplished.

Bratton's (2015) *The Stack* details the global Internet infrastructure as an ever-expanding accomplishment of the cooperation of militaries, universities, corporations, and municipalities across the globe. To give the matter the hyperbolic zing it deserves, one could point to Serres' (1990/1995) chalking the Internet up as a "world-object." World-objects are the culmination of objects' increasing range of actions and, recursively, the number of humans producing, using, and maintaining them. They are tools with dimensions commensurable to one of the dimensions of the world. In the case of the Internet, this dimension is space itself. Geert Lovink (2019) describes going offline and closing one's social media accounts as social death. "Just quitting" is not an option, and ensuring social inclusion is what keeps us "hooked."

Whether as a mode of work, play, or something else, somehow, online subjection appears to emanate from within the user, with little or no context. This stands in stark contrast to the form of interpellation described by Althusser (2014) and others which takes effect when a subject is hailed by a voice they understand to be calling out to them. It is this supposed shifted locus of control, from external enforcement (i.e. through prohibition) to internal self-expression and management that Deleuze (1992), in his infamous pages on the societies of control, calls "modulation." Deleuze and Guattari (1987, p. 435) define social formations by machinic processes of inscription. They claim that Marx's "modes of production" depend on these machinic processes which logically precede them. As an international organization that follows the capitalist axiomatic of de- and re-coding flows, Internet connectivity does not homogenize States and communities distant from its locale of origin. Rather, international organizations carry forward heterogeneous social formations that are isomorphic (insofar as they are diverse ways of realizing the capitalist axiomatic). These formations are brought together by both an external and an intrinsic coexistence of machinic processes (Deleuze & Guattari, 1987). The great veil of the digital age, at least where psychology is concerned, is the perpetual deferral of situated study of the actual social asymmetries fomented, exacerbated, recapitulated, and, in some instances, mitigated, in the churn of digital social networks.

Through advances in the post-Taylorism scientific management of human labor, control or "self-management" of users proceeds through data-driven advertising, marketing, surveillance, life optimization, self-quantification, and biohacking. From societies of discipline to societies of control, the historical passage from one to the next suggests that the "self" manages itself and that this is a more strict and insidious regime than the disciplining gaze of, for example, the panopticon. How can we interpret the functioning of control societies considering social media today? In what way does "the self" really subject itself to control processes? Control societies end up naming the computational intensity of interfaces and the governance of social life through the way that they coerce, divide, differentiate, provoke, assign, and remove permissions from users.

Given the spread of voices and personas that consider addiction to the Internet as a matter of concern, I suggest that we examine the affects of addiction to create what Haider (2018) calls an "insurgent universality." Taking cues from the Haitian slave uprisings under 18th-century French colonialism, insurgent universality refers to particular and concrete individuals and their political and social agency. Insurgent universality is not concerned with the rights-bearing individual in the abstract, but the universality of respect for formal incommensurability — a difference in itself. It urges that we are not to be reduced to victims. The users with whom we begin anticipate a reconfiguration based on their activity rather than passivity. Namely, their potential status as agents of the political demand of universal liberation — a liberation that is fought for individual selves "precisely because I [also] fight for that of the stranger" (p. 111).

While problematic as an individualizing, disciplinary technology of the psychological industry, the concept of addiction uniquely indexes many of the profundities of human subjectivity. The very notion of addiction enables us to locate subjectivity at the cusp of nature and culture, where we fold and incorporate elements of our milieu and unfold the ingenious and the unforeseen. The unbearable presence of *affects* — anger, jealousy, hatred, resentment, and confusion – control, time, and social forms are the vectors of a forthcoming critical psychology of users. Accounts of these deliver a series of new concepts in forging this crucially necessary facet of critical psychology of and for the digital era. The notion of control and its loss remains a core criterion for addictive disorders of all stripes (see Weinberg, 2013), despite the fact that the science of addiction lacks any successful means of distinguishing controlled drug use from the loss of self-control to drugs that is so pivotal to an addiction diagnosis (cf. Levine, 1978; Reinarman, 2005; Valverde, 1998; Volkow & O'Brien, 2007). The struggle for control and its flip side, submission, constitute the libidinal dialectic of digital subjects, inasmuch as it hearkens to a technological base beginning with language through which humans have the unique capacity to manipulate their surroundings, themselves, and each other. Correspondingly, dependence and powerlessness are affects (or cruelties) of Internet Addiction. Powerlessness as a cruelty of Internet Addiction is palpable in the manifest content of much of the web as hatred and as despair. Dependence, powerlessness, control, and compulsion are not confined to individual users but systematically distributed across users. This distribution gives rise to distinctive moments in the process of production and reproduction of the Internet *as* culture, where dependence, a sense of lost time, the creep of powerlessness, and pervasive anxiety double as techniques of social control *and* subjective catalysis.

A critical psychology of users must aim to collectivize "Internet Addiction," plucking it from the clinical context where it operates as a diagnostic category and placing its nominal force in the hands of those trying to rework a sense of autonomy and freedom in the networked world without any expectation of escaping from it entirely. If the Internet is a matter of concern, and the nomad-user, rather than the addict, an insurgent universal identification, there is good reason to suppose that an encounter between psychological institutions and ethical tech activists is imminent and fruitful. The relationship between psychological research, practice, and "user data" has historically served to delimit professional access to the psyche. Examining some possibilities afforded by the explosion in data collection and analysis of the "social web," I conclude by proposing a few ways that psychology could expand its (often sidelined) revolutionary practice of deep listening and self-critique to mitigate many obvious abuses of users by major web companies that are largely disinterested in the well-being of the latter. Despite the shortcomings of psychology's current handling of excessive Internet use, I sketch an optimistic program for its potential alliance with tech activists, scholars, and entrepreneurs who seek to remedy some of the most pernicious facets of the Internet we have today.

Psychology's voice could be a powerful asset for shifting the political economy of the Internet away from the competitive profit motive and toward cooperative alliance-building that I believe is the only hope of re-solving some of humanity's greatest challenges at present (of which constant Internet use is a *symptom* and a *fact* rather than a cause). Psychological in-stitutions are well-situated to advocate for personal data management di-vorced from profit-seeking, which will always make it a potent target for the exploitation of the population of all users, irrespective of relative excess or moderation. This is because psychologists uniquely understand the effects of the gaze, the difficulty of adapting to new societal configurations, and the self-other relations that are magnified and dramatically diminished in the online context. The pain of loss, envy, and the incessant drive toward mimetic competition and scapegoating, can only be made livable provided we have secure access to and a reasonable degree of genuinely collective control over the treasure trove that digital capitalists call personal data.

2
A BRIEF TAKE ON "INTERNET ADDICTION" IN PSYCHOLOGY

Stabilizing the motivational system in the name of reality

This chapter begins by looking at Internet Addiction through its symptomatology. Inquiring about its construction, it shares a brief historical narrative of the conceptual development of addiction, highlighting its conceptual moorings tied to the practice of psychologists and the formulation of psychological knowledge. What is called "addiction" has always intersected with the constitution of a pliable, susceptible individual, ready for subjection to a scientific regime of behavioral management geared toward stabilizing desire. Psychology's addictive disorder paradigm also increasingly maneuvers around thorny questions of desire, representation, and value by centering inquiry on the brain and cordoning off addictive behaviors from "real life" against which they are defined. Because it is a widely acknowledged, often definitive feature of modern culture, addiction to the Internet amplifies structural contradictions of the addictive paradigm and exemplifies the conceptual sloppiness of behavioral addictions. Specifically, it fails to distinguish between different uses and activities online and stops short of defining mechanisms of the Internet's addictiveness. This signals an inadequate grasp on the phenomenon it seeks to explain, which the rest of the piece seeks to remedy through a critical psychology of users.

The paradox of self-regulation found in neuroscientific and brain-based theories of addiction conveniently eschews specific historical developments and cultural adaptations to objects and behaviors that the addiction paradigm selectively moralizes. This is because focusing on the endogenous dopaminergic system as a motivational system locates something like an addictive capacity in human subjects, expanding the range of possible addictive "drugs," and extending the threat and verbiage of addiction to more people. These theories further suggest that brains, and by extension, human behavior, must continuously be monitored and regulated so that what is at root flexible and plastic can be kept stable. The call for the addict's stabilization through monitoring and reflexive regulation is particularly ironic in Internet Addiction, where the solution is logically indistinct from the workings of the drug; The solution and the fix both operate through the logic of reflexive networks.

Psychiatrist Ivan Goldberg coined the notion of "Internet addiction disorder" (IAD) satirically in the mid-1990s. After that point, it became picked up and targeted by mainstream media outlets as a severe source of social harm (Barnes & Pressey, 2014). Variously termed Internet Addictions, Technology Addictions, and Internet Gaming Disorders, they are only recognized for their likeness to other addictive substances on the basis of a perceived obsession, of which we must be wary "for its own sake." Simply put, researchers agree on the root definition, "excessive involvement in the Internet with negative consequences." Behavioral as opposed to substance disorders are defined, according to Black (2013), as disorders whose overt symptoms are visible to external observers, viewed at least initially as pleasurable, and attained the irresistible quality whose ascription in substance addictions is unquestionable. He says that the "boundaries of this emerging category are relatively fluid, appearing to expand or contract depending on an expert's own particular views" (p. 249).

Internet Addiction is a shifting entity moored by various institutional interests fearing the effects of the web and sensationalist accounts of massive social shifts in its wake. Internet Addiction is a behavioral addiction that subsumes in its own right a wide array of activities, the common denominator of which is the use of an Internet-enabled, or networked device. The taxonomic difficulties of experts do not, however, affect the intelligibility of Internet Addiction to non-psychologists. The pathological entity is so intelligible that participants self-reporting on their use habits needed practically no guidance in forming a sense of what constitutes excessive or problematic Internet use.

Block's (2008) model of Internet addiction includes the four components that consistently emerge to define behavioral addictions: excessive use, withdrawal, tolerance, and negative repercussions. These components, distilled from drug addictions for use across behavioral addictions, focus on the intensity of fascination. Epistemologically, they rely primarily on behavioral observation and secondarily on inferences drawn from affect with the drug-object as an independent variable. The notion of excessive use refers to the amount of time spent engaged in the usage behavior, and is frequently associated with loss of sense of time owing to the Internet's totally immersive qualities, and corresponds to high tolerance for its effects, implying the possibility that its grip can ramp up indefinitely for the involved user. Within Internet Addictions specifically, the loss of control comes from an altered temporality. The networked computer is construed as a technology of immersion whose special effect *as* a drug is an intoxication proper to hyper-focus. More specifically, the elevated levels of cognitive absorption experienced by some participants of virtual worlds create a state of "deep attention" (Snodgrass et al., 2011; Barnes & Pressey, 2014). Withdrawal symptoms include feelings of anger, tension, and depression when the user cannot engage in the activity, and negative repercussions like lying, underachievement, social isolation, fatigue, and decreased quality of the user's relationships.

Because behavioral addictions are entities created on the analogy of drug addictions, the state of the art of addiction science, in general, is relevant here. The dominant framework for the brain disease model of addiction is typified in the conception of addictive disorders given by the National Institute on Drug Abuse (see Courtwright, 2010). This institution heavily informs the addiction science used to develop diagnostic criteria. In this model, also widely referred to as the "disease model of addiction," it is argued that drugs cause biological euphoria by promoting the release of neurotransmitters, preventing their re-uptake, or mimicking their effects. Accordingly, extended use induces neurological adaptations that reduce users' sensitivity to alternative sources of reward and increase sensitivity to anticipated rewards of their drug of choice. The disease model, critics have pointed out, has congealed out of a long history of accounts into the current "official view" of addiction. This view is promulgated by state, corporate, and institutional interests that amassed in the evolution of addiction pathologies since its conceptual entanglement with illicit substances in the 19th century that created the need for a psycho-pharmaceutical industry for the treatment and governing of addicted subjects (Alexander, 2008; Hari, 2014; Maté, 2008).

Foucault (1965), among many others (see Levine, 1978) links the late-19th-century medico-juridical discourse of "toxicomania," an early iteration that would later become "addiction" and "addictive disorders," to the mania operating in the hierarchizing "science of types" that attempted to order the elements of the world by their supposed functions. The taxonomic impulse that characterized and formed these knowledge discourses placed addiction into the imagination of the late-19th-century welfare blend of medical, judicial, and social institutions. Many critically-minded characterizations of the current explosion of addiction pathologies highlight such top-down restraints on life, calling them "civilizing technolog[ies]" (Vrecko, 2010), and "medicalization[s] of deviance" (Schneider, 1978). Inspired primarily by Foucault's late work, Rose and other "governmentality theorists" (Rose, 2003, 2013; Valverde, 1998) draw attention to the productive normativity and governing rationalities issued through the science of addiction as it increasingly centers on the brain.

The question of whether addiction is a disease is now overshadowed by the consensus that it is a cerebral phenomenon. The hegemonic narrative of addictions in the field more broadly is that addiction is a pathology of the dopaminergic system, and drugs are said to metaphorically "hijack" this system. Levy's (2013) "Addiction is not a brain disease" attests to this eclipse, even while being ostensibly interested in the disease question. One finds in this paper that one should err on the side of compassion (read: not a disease) because the neural dysfunction to which addiction points is not sufficient for impairment (where impairment is a necessary condition for the disease label). Instead, it is a pathology of the midbrain dopamine system. The midbrain dopamine system is a valuation system, or a reward prediction system (see also Montague et al., 1996; Schultz, 1997). Accordingly, its role is to signal the value of a resource to the organism and motivate it toward a level of consumption that will aid its survival and reproduction.

According to Catharine Malabou (2012), neuroscience has successfully replaced "sexuality" with "cerebrality," a concept that denotes the specific causality of the brain, hormones, and neurons for all affects. The dominance of neuroscientific cerebrality and its dazzling images of the human brain nevertheless effect a trajectory through which the endogenous opioid system – auto-erotic capacity is discovered (Trigo et al., 2010). The Freudian notion of libido, for example, is replaced by the notion of "appetites," as in the Excessive Appetites Theory (Orford, 2001). The Excessive Appetites Theory of Addiction (Orford, 2001) gives an explanatory model of how any object or activity can put humans at risk of developing a strong attachment. It touts improvement upon other models of addiction – those whose accounts are unable to situate the becoming-addicting of any and all things over and above substances manufactured to dominate the human body chemically. The theory is accommodating in its move toward unifying disparate and seemingly contradictory effects of dependence under a radically "ecological" model – personality, biochemistry, the surrounding environment, and the drug itself is equally at play in the development of an addiction. These elements are knotted together through a disorder of the *motivational system* at large. This system is a chaotic one, undergirded by the fashionable notion of the brain's flexible, radically adaptable character. Through it, one learns that the motivational system has evolved to be inherently unstable:

> The motivational system is built like a "fly-by-wire" aircraft with built in instability that requires constant balancing input to keep it "on the straight and narrow". This has the advantage of making us highly adaptive and creative but the disadvantage that, without balancing inputs, including devices and techniques to stabilize our mental processes, we readily develop maladaptive thought processes and behaviour patterns.
>
> *(West & Brown, 2013, p. 5)*

In these theories, the whole of the human motivational system is understood to be so fragile and susceptible to unwanted intrusion that it requires constant balancing. The need for perpetual balancing delineates a form of the subject, including and beyond addicts, for whom the question of self-control is perpetually looming and whose creativity and adaptability are strangely liable to morph into their opposite – that is, in the absence of stabilizing devices and techniques. Note the knitting of body and environment happens in the brain, whose capacity to adapt is equally a blessing and a curse – its very nature requires that humans supplement their motivational systems with devices and techniques that keep what Freud first called *der Trieb* (the drive) "on the straight and narrow." Perhaps the increasing scope of addiction may be viewed either as the becoming-addictive or the addictive capacities behind or beneath objects and behaviors that were never thought to be so, and as the increasing capacity of subjects to become addicted to anything, or to enact infinite "misrepresentations of value."

Conceiving addiction as a problem of an individual brain's ability to represent value in the environment to itself is an exceedingly clever rhetorical tactic. When Eve Sedgwick (1993), charted the logic underpinning the boom of addictions in psychology, she found that its conceptual and practical slippage suggests different loci of addictiveness – neither the substance nor the body. She concluded that this must entail some abstraction that would settle the narration of relations between the two. The abstraction that determines Eve Sedgwick's subject-object question that underpins the notion of addiction is revealed to be the brain as a faulty mediator. Where addiction science used to expend efforts adjudicating between the user and the drug, it now suggests that what connects them is problematic. In this way, there is nothing wrong with a drug object "in itself," nor is a person to blame for their shortcomings, their circumstances, their biology, etc. The body of the user, with its neurotransmitters, adrenaline, and cortisol, take on an increased role in controlling consumption *qua* uptake of the consumed. Still, the mediating, representational brain requires techniques and devices for its stabilization. Sedgwick's piece also links the anti-sodomitic discourse that bore early witness to the binary opposition of that which is natural and that which is unnatural, with the perhaps lineal 21st-century discourses on substances and behaviors on the basis of a distinction between natural desires called "needs" and artificial desires called "addictions." Where squeamishness with respect to broaching the enjoying body once made the distinction between "natural" and "artificial" rewards clear, endogenous opioids emitted from the brain place the pleasures (and also the horrors) associated with addiction within the brain as an inadequate information processor, and therefore also unfit to perceive and deliberate as a representative of (and within) a human being.

This move involves the effort of researchers, across nearly all fields of study, increasingly relying on computers as tools to map relations between data, representing aspects of human thought that would otherwise remain unobservable. The most widely funded studies on humans are typically in neuroscience, where conceptual innovation relies on ever more creative applications of computation to elicit new neurological data. And in mental health contexts, computational models of mental disorders are now being positioned as viable alternatives to conventional diagnostic taxonomies, like the DSM (Adams et al., 2016). These new models collect data about individuals' mental, social, and biological lives to plug them into network modeling programs that map data-constellations in ways that can continually be updated as more data is collected on service users. Could it be that Psychology swung from the libido and sexuality to cerebrality on the basis of the new way of seeing afforded by the network technologies that, in this particular instance, it seeks to problematize?

Locating addiction in a faulty system of cerebral representation justifies treatments that plunge more deeply into the body (the brain), obfuscating the collective nature of enjoyment and its representation as an act to be undertaken by the user-subject (rather than extrapolated by the firings of its neurons or the behaviors of its body). This largely precludes the possibility that the fact of an addiction may be used to question the presence of the drug in the environment of the user, naturalizing the social systems of a drug's production, distribution, and exchange. For these theories, it is instead the relationship between internality and externality that should be balanced and stabilized by techniques and devices, subjecting this relation to the foregone conclusion that already-existing misrepresentation is met with psy-industrial management. On this account, the pathology of addiction is a problem of the in-between – a problem of information. The hubris of science that claims to be able to register a mismatch between the value that a subject assigns to an object and the actual value of the object for the subject is breathtaking in its paternalism.

In this model, the brain is called upon as a representative or liaison to the interpretive expertise of psychologists, making value judgments on behalf of the whole person, protecting their interests, and acting for their benefit. The human body is treated as a microcosm of a representative democracy with its own central spokesperson in charge of relaying the decisions of the whole. The correspondence between this rhetoric of addiction science and the rhetoric of centrally-managed markets extends even beyond the normal sense in which theorists of addiction sound like amateur economists (choices, rewards, and incentives, oh my!), trying to tweak price signals to solicit a match between market offerings – that which *should* be desirable – and the desiring subject. This turn to managing the brain reflects the struggle embodied in the neoliberal subject of the market, in that the optimal functioning of this subject presupposes adequate information about choices (which are not always available). As Foucault (2007) says, the market becomes the "grid of intelligibility," and the self-as-human-capital integrates the body securely into this grid. The claim to know a mismatch between the value assigned to an object by a subject and its actual value *for the subject* is provocative, not least because "value" is among the most elusive of concepts in capitalism. More importantly, it gives lie to this free market subject by exposing the degree to which its desire is molded, modulated, managed, and corrected all in the name of its true or real desire.

The addict's brain unreliably represents or gives false information that psychological aid comes to fill in, even as it also contains the key to the hidden calculus of the endogenous opioid system. It is as if it is the job of neuroscience's techniques and devices to reveal the brain's auto-erotic knowledge to itself. These expert tools possess this key that would unlock, finally, a truly harmonious relationship between subject and object, based in transparent communication of what is really on offer. In the case of addiction neuroscience, with its slapdash application to the Internet notwithstanding, the brain reflects, primarily, the needs of the social institution (s) that theorize it. The conclusion here is that, in its role as an economic advisor to the body, addiction neuroscience gives its subjects lifestyle techniques and tips for a more true or real calculus for the maximization of pleasure divorced from the active, living force of desire.

Malabou's (2012) proclaimed substitution of sexuality for cerebrality has created conditions within which the anti-social dangers of enjoyment justify submitting the so-called addict to a regime of normality achieved by intensive forms of monitoring and modulating. One could conclude that, where addiction is concerned, psychology's shift from sexuality to cerebrality is one that moves a potential interest in the social and economic configuration of objects of enjoyment and subjects who enjoy toward the calculation of value in the environment by the brain. For the addict and the purpose of pathology, this has the effect of shunting, into the private domain of the individual, concerns that illuminate and problematize the functioning of the entire socio-economic apparatus. The medicalization of addiction that proceeds by locating the problem in the brain is far simpler and more convenient to a treatment industry that separates individuals, severs them from their contexts and attempts to fix them one-by-one, reproducing the alienating effects of the problem to which the treatment is at least partially summoned to respond.

Even while disorders of the addictive brain are specified in great detail, the human subject of Internet Addiction is surprisingly abstract. A large part of the problem with the formulation of Internet Addiction in Psychology is a strong disinterest on behalf of psychologists in what is happening to the user of the Internet. Psychological theories of addiction handle IA through an implicit de-realization of digital, networked technologies for lack of other models through which to explain the effects of these technologies. Studies of habitual Internet use under the banners of addictive, problematic, or unregulated behavior do not even bother to distinguish between different types of online activities (see Young & Rogers, 1998; Caplan, 2005; LaRose et al., 2003). Amidst a total lack of conceptual rigor, apparent problems related to Internet use slosh together under the dominance of a model whose reputation precedes it: addiction. So, poor, problematic, excessive, or addictive Internet habits all figure in together as substitutions for other, lost activities, or compensation for competence in other activities (like socializing per se). Caplan's (2005) "social skills" account explicitly frames excessive Internet use as a form of compensation for social skills that it deems "real world." Aligned with the self-regulatory deficits to which psychology credits the brain directly, substitutions for the real world are related to deficient processes of self-observation: awareness, attention, control, and intention. This de-realization parallels the story of dopaminergic activities that raise tolerance, requiring higher and higher doses or increased time and resulting in the automaticity of habit.

The diagnostic category Internet Addiction and related discursive formulations of problematic and excessive Internet use impede rather than heighten comprehension of the phenomenon of non-stop Internet connectivity and the massive increase in digitally-mediated communication, primarily through repetition of the wedge between the Internet and another world that is more real. The way that Internet Addiction, like other addictive disorders, takes care to make wasted time into a key diagnostic consideration is exemplary. According to Johnson & Keane (2015), a large part of the implicit ideal of controlled consumption in the psychopathological concept of addiction is a particular understanding of time. Whatever means by which addiction is said to "hijack" the dopaminergic system and the life of the user is expressed in the misuse or mismanagement of time. The most recent diagnostic and statistical manual, the DSM-V, lends credence to this characterization of addiction in which the enslavement at stake is not to an enigmatic, alluring object, but rather to a problematic experience of time. Problematic in its discordance with the hegemony of whatever aspects of life the habit forecloses or makes difficult. One of the diagnostic criteria of addictive disorders is that "a great deal of time" is spent obtaining and using the substance or recovering from its effects (APA, 2013, p. 483). Nie (2001) and LaRose et al. (2011), also explains the negative effects of the Internet in terms of "time inelasticity," where the sheer quantity of time spent on the Internet is problematic in that it displaces other activities, where displacement itself is the problem: a rather conservative perspective! Use of the Internet is generally pitted against quotidian life, and an addictive habit is recognizable once a hierarchy of priorities shifts such that "daily activities" revolve around substance use rather than the other way around (ibid).

The Internet is defined negatively rather than positively, qualified only as a potent enough distraction for the user to lose track of "real life," setting up a false binary where net-related activities are pitted against things that matter. The utility of the Net, or more accurately, its lacking utility, is a foregone conclusion. Yet, at root, this de-realization is a simple categorization of an activity, Internet use, as *useless*. And not only is this activity useless, but it is also de-personalizing. It dissimulates our notion of an individual as forged through meaningful activity, meaningful relationships, meaningful ownership, and meaningful civic participation. It robs us of control, intention, attention, and self-awareness exposing through omission that these are requirements of non-pathological (normal) human subjects. Hidden also beneath mesmerizing neuroscientific correlations between the stimulation of various areas of the brain and use of the Internet is a punitive dismissal of the flight *from* an individual so constructed toward something *else*. The discursive and imagistic construction of addiction is of a piece with the task of psychological theory, historically the terrain of intellectuals describing and managing the social system through its claim to knowledge of the individuals who make it up (Parker, 1999). This construction, therefore, governs knowledge used to manage, control, and discipline subjects, reproducing them along genealogical lines and their coordinates of race, sex, gender, nationality, and class.

Adapting any and all things to the model of addiction provisioned by illicit substances proceeds through survey data that testifies to the subject's excessive engagement with "X" and treatment options that are agnostic about the specific effects of particular drugs, again, homogenizes them through the assumption of the idiosyncratic, unknowable brain of the addict, whose creativity and adaptability silently selects loci of pleasure that mental health professionals must nominate and regulate, retroactively, as such. In this key, the expansion and contraction of addiction pathologies do not only regulate enjoyment for particular subjects. Nor is the influence of pathologies in the making limited to widespread stigmatization of particular areas of human devotion (though this happens rather easily when the nascent "Internet Addiction" is itself legitimized through correlation with better established mental illnesses like depression and anxiety (e.g. Bernardi & Palanti, 2009; Saikia et al., 2019). These correlations are made on top of the already dubious analogy to drug addictions on which behavioral addictions are entirely based (e.g. Davis, 2001).

In contraposing addictive enjoyment to the business of real life, and casting human effort and attention as problematic behavior, pathological addiction framings are complicit in blocking new areas of activity *as* matters of concern with which to engage. The flexible de-realization of activity, its separation from real life has implications for what parts of human activity are to be counted as valuable. In the case of social media, which we will explore in great depth, addictification adds an authorial voice to obfuscation and historical lack of value attributed to the aesthetic dimensions of subjectivity and the reproduction of social relations through care. Moreover, relegating technology to an object of addiction divorced from real-life fails to recognize the sense in which it is an engine for the development of material production (which more apparently forms the basis of all social life) (Marx, 1867/1990, p. 286). In the following section, we explore what it entails to mount a critical psychology of the user based on the productivity of desire rather than on a substitution for or deviation from life.

Digital non-duality is one way to approach the increasing confluence of real-life and digital technologies that enables an overcoming of the psychological pitting of "real life" against net-connected device usage. Digital non-duality bespeaks the impossibility (and detriment) of making hard and fast distinction between life online and life offline, as it obscures the way in which our networked world operates and belittles its recursive effects on the organization and production of subjectivity. It, therefore, obfuscates the connection between networked technologies and political, economic, and social realities to which we are becoming accustomed. The risk we run in taking for granted how social reality is constructed through network technologies is losing the imagination and will to reconstruct it differently. To put it simply, we are neglectful and skittish about the sorts of changes we are undergoing as a society because most facets of life have some networked component or have been affected by digital infrastructures that change our habits, ways of relating to each other, and ways of moving about the world. The problem with psychology's rendering of dependence on the Internet through its addiction paradigm is that it *doesn't go far enough* in explaining the strange sense of inevitability shrouding digital life by way of either the desire of users or the machinations of global capitalism. It risks instead making spectacles or even scapegoats of individual human beings mired, by way of specific subjective coordinates in formation, in society's dependence on digital infrastructures and network protocols.

The way psychology handles IA is symptomatic of its own venture: Creating the abstraction, "the average net user," it was about ten years after its initial formulation that researchers began to insist that studies on the matter would do well to focus on specific Internet activities rather than taking the entirety of Internet use for granted (e.g. LaRose et al., 2011; Starcevic & Aboujaoude, 2017). Yet, it is certain that those who use the Internet excessively and perhaps suffer in doing so increasingly have a life entwined with the Internet – and that this applies to more and more of us. Beyond the pleasure-and-peril model of the Internet implied by its addictification by psychology and related disciplines, however, we might consider "Internet Addiction" an expression of concern over a feature of society that becomes increasingly structural with every passing year. This is most evident amid social distancing requirements of the novel coronavirus pandemic when Internet use represents the most important opportunities for social life. If indeed, we cannot quit being online, we must consider why this is the case without the baggage of psychology's specific, Western hegemonic notions and requirements about what it is to be human.

During an era of profound technological development and dependence, "Internet Addiction" is also a discursive object, or a signifier pointing to the social struggle for control over technology writ large. The framing of digital technologies as objects of addiction parallels the way conservative politicians blame smartphones and social media platforms for uprisings caused by social inequality, poverty, and systemic racism, such as the Arab Spring, Occupy Wall Street, and Black Lives Matter demonstrations. Fuchs (2014) points out that panics over social media are a new phase in the history of moral panics that abstracts from societal causes of problems, favoring instead casting blame on a technology whose affordances make expressions of outrage and discontent possible. At the time of this writing, Donald Trump is threatening to take down social media platform, Twitter, for bias against conservative voices – another attempt to blame the technology for popular outrage over his authoritarian regime.

Here, I propose a new understanding of Internet Addiction as a shared recognition or sociality based upon and taking place within the habitual social, economic, and political cycles upon which all users depend and in the face of which are, ultimately, powerless. It is not a "virtual" addiction in distinction from an "actual" addiction, like an addiction to drugs. Neither is it a "virtual" addiction as opposed to an "actual" addiction, like an addiction to something that is other than the electronic screen (the only thing common to all the "kinds" that fit under the "category" IA: smartphone addiction, social media addiction, online gambling or shopping addiction, television addiction). Since the early 2000s, Lacanian psychoanalysts have been quick to point out that cyberspace, as it was called then, radicalizes the gap constitutive of the symbolic order of society, which is "always already" virtual. In essence, the claim is that any access to social reality must be supported by an implicit fantasmic hypertext (Parker, 2007; Žižek 1999). It is a virtual addiction in a minimal and specific sense: it is a compulsion toward the dominant mode of sociality, which has always been the virtual, which is to say, an addicted relationship to the conceptual edifice of sociality itself: information, data, language, communication, writing, electronic media, journalism, etc. As (Starcevic & Aboujaoude, 2017) succinctly put the matter, one cannot be addicted to a medium or a delivery device without specifying the mechanisms that make it addictive. This has not, to date, been studied before, and is a large part of what this piece tries to understand.

There is instead dependence on something we might package together and call "culture." This is quite simple to say, to our humanness. Reflecting on Nietzsche's 19th-century retort to Rousseau's extensive idealization of the human being during the Enlightenment, Bard and Soderqvist (2018) remark that before the genesis of culture, there is nothing of value save a gaping hole of animist emptiness. In short, without culture, we humans are nothing. Internet Addiction must then be understood as what it is: A pathologizing of culture itself, in the spirit of classical, Freudian psychoanalysis that always sought to point out the pathological in the normal and the hyper-extended normal within the pathological. It is fine to bemoan culture but refusing to consider what it consists of is a grave problem for clinical work with Internet Addicts to come. The extent to which psychopathology and mental health diagnoses turn quickly into sources of authoritative guide points for the generation of common knowledge and sense-making (online especially, as it goes) supports this admonition.

3

SCHIZOANALYSIS, TECHNOLOGY, AND SOCIALITY

Technology through the lens of schizoanalysis

Another framing of culture, one which focuses on its construction and inventiveness, is the selective process of marking or inscription "that invents the large numbers in whose favor it is exerted" (p. 343). The writings of Deleuze and Guattari help explore how the network society in which we now live, like all civilizations, have as their concomitant discontent, an indifference to the individual user on which it is ostensibly modeled, and a tendency to express enjoyment as a function of the socius taken as a whole.

In contrast to the psychological understanding of the Internet as a reified object of addiction to which individuals are vulnerable, Deleuzo-Guattarian *schizoanalysis* provides a conceptual basis for understanding digital technologies as processes of capitalist social development constitutive of social relations moved continuously by a global collective of users. A reading of the Internet and/as social media, energized by an interwoven look at the four theses of schizoanalysis, sets up an examination of the processual dynamics of the social media machine as a collective assemblage of enunciation. This assemblage articulates humans and digital technologies together to show how these assemblages individualize users from a constitutive global, collectivity not conscious of the collective power that is the productive force of their desires. This chapter concludes by revisiting the notion of getting hooked in terms of the mass migration achieved by net-connected technologies: Online, but also across borders, and into and out of informal, often economic, networks that further enmesh and invest users socially in digital systems.

This is a lot to unpack and requires a few different arguments. The first is that, as Deleuze and Guattari (1986) explain, people are never enslaved to *technical* machines, but rather to social machines. Technical machines, like the devices to which we are ostensibly addicted, are a residue of desiring-machines or human organisms in their capacity for language, symbolism, and abstraction. It is this human technology which precedes material technologies. While the latter develops effects across the entirety of the social field, particular tools and technical machines are taken up by machinic social assemblages (Deleuze, 1988, p. 39). There is no technological determinism here, nor technological neutrality. Instead, all technologies are simultaneously technical and social means that their invention and deployment parallel and reflect the values and material interests of social groups. Guattari (2013) gives the example of a clock, which can be explained through the lens of technical machines because it measures uniform time. A clock can also be viewed as a social machine, too, in that it reproduces canonical hours to assure order in a city.

The dual aspects of technical and social machines exemplify how humans figure into broader "machining" processes whereby they link up with other agents of all stripes to form functional constellations of matter — yet *other* machines, in chaotic, emergent, and interdependent social production. Social machines have people for parts, even if we view them with their technical machines. So, the social machine fashions a memory without which there would be no synergy of human and (technical) machines. Technical machines do not contain the conditions for their reproduction, but they do point to social machines that organize them, while at the same time limiting and extending their development. While the difference between a social and technical machine is perspectival, the distinction is important for getting our bearings in considering the human-machine entanglement that, while always having existed, comes to the fore today all the more plainly, configuring social life and pressing us to define our humanity in and against its automatic, calculative operations. Social machines, like multiple levels of state and transnational governments, court systems, trade agreements, patents, landed property owners, environmental agencies, resource management systems, in short, all of the institutions that affected us before its development continue to organize, support, and condition its new uses and directions.

Technical machines, then, gesture toward a social and biological mastery and control. They take their cues from Marx's methodological focus on the productive organs of man in society, which form the material basis of different social organizations (Marx, 1981). Technical machines are traditionally understood to imply a transmitting or driving nonhuman element that extends human strength and allows for a certain disengagement. Deleuze and Guattari go farther than this, echoing Samuel Butler to assert that technical machines are limbs and organs of society that are appropriated based on power and wealth (1986, p. 284). Inevitably, this leaves the impoverished deprived *as if they are mutilated, limbless, and organ-less*. Despite this profound statement about access to technology as a means of growing or depleting social power, the two had no interest in comparing humans and machines such that the two could become extricable or conceived in terms of competition with each other. On the contrary, the perspective offered here suggests that individualizing the struggle between humans and technology creates another degree of separation between humans struggling against each other with technologies that do not belong to anyone in particular (the first degree being human groups struggling against technologies themselves).

While machines do not determine different types of society, they are easily matched with them because they are expressive of the social forms that generate and use them (Deleuze 1992, p. 6). Likewise for Marx, "technology reveals the active relation of man to nature, the direct process of the production of his life, and thereby it also lays bare the process of the production of the social relations of his life, and of the mental conceptions that flow from those relations (Harvey & Marx, 2010, p. 192). When he used the word "technology" interchangeably with "productive forces," he bundled together social-organizational forms and technical machines, which is quite apropos considering the goal of social organization that appears *for its own sake* on social media (Harvey & Marx, 2010). This "for its own sake" morphs into numerous overlapping, non-coincident contexts that it nevertheless brings together as if to resolve the contradictory roles that were more spatially and temporally distinctive in earlier social forms.

Contra the metaphorical use of the notion of machines, Deleuze and Guattari hypothesized that a process of machining could apply to any element through recursive communication and feedback loops. This is a transdisciplinary idea called *cybernetics,* which we explain in more depth below. For now, suffice to say that the above implies that the production of civilization itself is machinic. Guattari remarks that each machine produces a new civilization through the "invention of writing, technological innovation, and the introduction of a division of labor" that usually receive a jumpstart by military machines that, in capitalist societies, and arguably before, initiate an ongoing process of innovations that seek the maximally efficient use of labor and machines (1984; 2015, p. 178). He adds that behind each of these civilizational mutations lies a loss of control by signifying chains that give way to incoherent and short-term semiotics in anticipation of a new plane of reference that is also structured like a language. He is suggesting that the modern civilization materializes upon replacement of the old signifying chains and references.

The socius in Deleuze and Guattari is a full body that creates a surface of the recording of production. As a second nature, processes of production seem to emanate from this very recording surface as its divine presupposition. The socius is a recording surface that naturalizes production based on its recording capacity. A social machine is literally a machine when it exhibits an "immobile motor" and operates interventions like setting flows apart, detaching elements from a chain, and portioning and distributing tasks. Coding flows implies all these subsequent operations. Therefore, the division between a signifier and what it signifies and that between subjects and objects are the same. On this basis, excessive or addictive relations with technological objects cannot be understood as a force of anti-sociality. They must instead assume a place within the socio-technical production.

The first thesis of schizoanalysis is that every investment is social and bears upon a sociohistorical field. For mental health professionals, Internet Addiction constitutes a strong investment or attachment of the libido (or in neuroscientific terminology, an appetite). From that perspective, it is precisely antisocial insofar as it removes the user-addict from an [implicitly] *real* or at least a more real social world within which they should be participating. Conversely, from a schizoanalytic perspective, investment is social because it is productive of the socius itself. Addiction to the Internet concerns us all, not least because anyone reading this book likely found it on the Internet. We are implicated in the (social and socializing) Internet. In this sense, it is perhaps a misstep to begin developing a critical psychology of users and the qualities of "the drug," through the canonical, disciplinary lens of Psychology's attempts to manage the enjoyment of the Internet. Such management is even more transparent considering the grafting of the signifier "addiction" onto a wide variety of different substances and behaviors. The Internet, in its particularity, however, attests to real social development *as* a productive economy of desire. A critical psychology of users, therefore, requires a *positive, descriptive* understanding of Internet use rather than assuming its role and meaning (e.g. "a distraction," a "nuisance," a form of social maladaptation) in a user's life from the outset.

Social forms

In *Anti-Oedipus*, different assemblages of desiring-production are situated historically upon the full body of the Earth, the Despot, or Capital. About the full bodies of the different modes of the socius, the pair writes,

If we wonder where these forms of force come from, it is evident that they are not to be explained in terms of any goal or end, since they are what determine goals and ends. The form or quality of any given socius — the body of the earth, the despot, or the body of capital-money — depends on a state or degree of intensive development of the productive forces, insofar as these forces define a man–nature independent of all the social formations, or rather common to them all (what the Marxists term the "givens of useful labor"). The form or quality of the socius is therefore itself produced, but as the unengendered — that is, as the natural or divine precondition of production corresponding to a given degree to which it affixes a structural unity and apparent goals, those which it falls back, and whose forces it appropriates, thereby determining the selections, the accumulations, and the attractions without which these forces would not assume a social character.

(1986, p. 343).

Socialization equates to codification, and it is the business of the socius to desire and to delay (or fear) as much as possible the decoding of flows through the organs it develops. Pre-capitalist social machines, then, are recapitulated in the way that the flows of desire are coded. Such a hypothesis assumes that desire is gregarious in nature, and that desire needs to be trained to be made lasting in the collective. Hence coding. They hypothesize that capitalism as de-coding was known to the primitive peoples as that which would destroy their society and their rituals were designed to preserve them from this menace. Capitalism is the negation of all social formations and overtly inimical to them. Precapitalist forms were solely interested in se-curing the coding of elements, making sure nothing slipped by, and therefore were occupied primarily with the purpose of reproducing them-selves. This is to say that they were not aiming to create a surplus. Their objective, therefore, was embedded, clear as day, into labor as the fulfillment of need as they defined them across time for generations. Capitalism, con-trary to other social machines, is constructed based on decoded flows, wherein an axiomatic of abstract quantities (in the money form) are sub-stituted for intrinsic codes. While flows of desire seem liberated, such lib-eration is followed by control and modulation of desire through the recoding of flows in accordance with the capitalist axiomatic.

Anti-Oedipus further specifies that capitalism provides the conditions for universal history by celebrating the decoded flows that have haunted every form of society prior to it. It is perhaps most clear in the chapter of *What is Philosophy?* on Geophilosophy, where Marx's construction of the concept of capitalism exemplifies philosophy as abstract-real thought that cannot confirm the materiality of its movement without immediately becoming political philosophy (Alliez et al., 2010). Guattari indicated this potential in the way he understood the dominant mode of power in the present day. For Deleuze and Guattari, these cultural apparatuses make possible the historical contextualization of the inscription, and thus the qualities and problematics, and the mode of operation, of the body without organs. The body of the addict as a body of decoded flows, always susceptible to the next supplement and for that very reason needing to be kept on the straight-and-narrow, is demonstrative of flexible coding on the basis of the celebration of decoded flows. The way objects are situated in light of such a celebration is through an axiomatic, immanent logic of de- and re-territorialization (Deleuze & Guattari, 1976).

Guattari (2013) claims that regardless of the succession of its avatars, the drive that inheres in capitalism has always knotted together a de-territorializing component (that leads to the destruction of social territories, collective identities, and traditional systems of value), and an artificial recomposition, escalating to greater and greater degrees of tragic/comic transparency, of individuated personological frameworks, schemes of power, and models of submission. The latter, also called re-territorializations or re-codings, are functionally if not formally similar to whatever they are supposed to be replacing. The ever-expanding interior edge of capitalism establishes itself upon the decoding of former social systems, whittling these down to raw materials inputs for new productive cycles (Culp, 2019). Deterritorialization, as it was developed in Anti-Oedipus, comes from a reading of Marx, in that it supports a "universal history" whose contingent movements can only be understood from the new decoding and cooperative necessities of capitalism. To this end, political philosophers in the Deleuzo-Guattarian tradition call for fine-tuned analyses of the relation between deterritorialization and reterritorialization as they operate in particular assemblages, and how these relate to the "ultimate" reterritorialization onto the axiom of profit and capital growth.

The absolute productivity of desire

The insular form of desire to which addiction normally refers applies itself to "the social," against which psychologists frame this desire as pathological. The subject of addiction in psychology, is an Oedipal subject, according to Deleuze and Guattari. The western, liberal individual "I" of privation is a subject who can be understood to *own* their desire, just as personhood in the occidental context involves a self-possession or ownership of one's body (as to be able to sell its productive capacity as labor in the capitalist market).

Yet, one might rightly raise an eyebrow at an interpretation of addiction in which "individual" desire is understood apart from or out of line with the social in the context of addiction *to the dominant locus of sociality today*. Where the disciplinary formation of Internet Addiction understands the desire proper to the Internet as a sacrifice or deferral of social life, we see here the deep, mutual implication of society and desiring-production; for Internet Addiction, this is all the more clear, as we sink ever deeper into a regime of ubiquitous communication.

Within the canon of psychoanalytic and post-psychoanalytic theory, there is a strong body of work supporting two co-extensive ideas. The first is that enjoyment is not private but is already highly socialized. It presupposes an entire artifice of codes and norms conditioned by the rhythms of expectation vis-a-vis dispositions of the body. The second is that enjoyment is productive; it is not only an active, living force, but it can be (and is) put to work, at the service of the reproduction of society. Lacan will guide us through the first, reasoning from the individual body to its social formation. Deleuze and Guattari, with their reinvigoration of the Marxian categories of labor, production, and technical and social machines work the opposite; reasoning from the fiber optic cables and technical protocols that are the Internet to its functioning as a social machine, and its "use" of individual bodies producing "content" that operate as its inputs.

Enjoyment relates to the energetic aspect of Freud's drive theory, and it is the body that experiences it, as it is variously connected to tension (Lacan, 1966/2006). Enjoyment (*jouissance*) in Lacan's work gives name to the ineffable energetics, the often destructive, unexpected, jarring *beyond* of the pleasure principle that regulates it. The latter might be said only to indicate the necessity of detours from the path by which the subject is sustained along the search for enjoyment. The drive-ridden body, as the body that enjoys, has a contentious role in psychoanalysis more broadly. Lacan may be more popularly read as having issued the reality of the body as imaginary, particularly in light of his popular formulation of the "mirror stage" when the nascent subject is able to identify with his whole image in the mirror. While it is undoubtedly the case that one's reflection is saturated by the significations and norms of the culture it exists in, the body is not *only* the image constructed by the symbolic. The drive-ridden body is subject to symptoms, and far from being imaginary, it hosts libido and enjoyment. The real body of psychoanalysis is that which enjoys itself, and, as Lacan says, we don't know what it means to be alive except that a body is something that enjoys itself (as cited in Soler, 2016).

This body is further formed and reformed through the rhythms of its changing dispositions, considering enjoyment as a real force and the semblances of its distribution, management, and image. As Lacan (2002) says in seminar XIV, "the locus of the Other ... designated the locus of the Other in the body" (p. 141). His point is that it would be impossible for the body *not* to be the locus of the Other – this body is, in effect, the writing pad of the Other. Late in his teaching, Lacan situates enjoyment in his theory of the discourses, giving it a somewhat different flavor. In this context, enjoyment is defined as the disturbing dimension in the experience of being a body. Being a body is revealed to be disturbing precisely as far as one's experience with enjoyment conveys the truth of non-self-sufficiency to the subject. This is because, as Alenka Zupančič (2017) succinctly puts it:

> enjoyment and the Other are structured like a matryoshka: enjoyment is "in" the Other, but when we look "in" the enjoyment, there is also the Other "in" it, and so on. ... Enjoyment is in the Other, and the Other is in enjoyment – This is perhaps the most concise formulation of the structure of the non-relation, the non-relation between the subject and the Other. If enjoyment is what disturbs this relation, it does so not simply by coming between them (and hence holding them apart), but rather by implicating, placing them one in the other. (p. 29)

The notion of Internet Addiction fetishizes the technological machine, suggesting that the great pull of the technology itself creates the conditions sufficient for addiction. It does not. Rather, it is the fantastic pull of the Other and its interlocking with enjoyment that makes engagement on social platforms irresistible. Not only are pathologies of enjoyment guilty of mirroring the same device fetishism they condemn; the same move inches psychological theorists dangerously close to pathologizing, in broad daylight, the joy of sociality, and thus also the collective power to which its creation of individuals has always aimed to chip away. Psychology's unintentional complicity in this fetishism reconstitutes the artificial separation of humans and gadgets from the entire social machine of which they act together as inputs. Meanwhile, the device, rather than the social relations it congeals, becomes the object of allure rather than those relations in their specificity. For Deleuze and Guattari, the machine is to be grasped in immediate relation to a social body and not at all to a human biological organism. Both humans and tools are already machine parts on the full body of the respective society. Psychological formulations of addiction sustain a misnomer about the nature of enjoyment that makes such pathological kinds infinitely flexible instruments for stigmatization and de-legitimation of human activity. While distributed through the psychological language of

addiction, the misnomer, clearly visible in its direct rendering of pathological enjoyment, has important ramifications for economic subjects, the
optics of their participation, and the agency implied in their individual and
collective power.

If it is possible to re-appropriate addictions to the internet (particularly
social media) from its punitive context within the psy-industries, one could
reframe it as addiction to inscription alongside the capitalist axiomatic,
which increasingly de- and re-territorializes data traces. While the migration
of human bodies may be the decisive human issue of the era of ecological
and climate-related catastrophe, the only thing we can say for certain about
users is that they *compulsively subject themselves* to the Internet. This compulsive auto-subjection is of a piece with and attests to, desire's investment
of the social field. American users spend countless hours on their smartphones and in front of other screens each day, with nearly a third reporting
to the Pew Research Center in 2019 that they are online constantly. Other
awe-inspiring usage statistics collected by private companies across the web
relay that people open up their phones fifty-eight times a day on average or
that over eighty percent of adults use the Internet daily, providing charts that
show years of individual lives spent on social media. To say that we are all
addicts or excessive users is to recognize that we are all within the changing
regime of social machines, and thus in a similarly complicit position vis-a-vis
the re-territorializing axiomatic of capital. It is more accurate to say that the
whole network constituting one or more social media platforms *is* an
addiction, rather than supposing that an individual *has* an addiction.

Addiction is not only the way psychology understands the technological
hybridity of subjectivity (see Haraway, 1991), but the sheer fact of its intelligibility in the context of the DSM reflects and may even end up am-
plifying the already dominant, misguided attitudes toward technology. The
addiction framework situates the user as the human consumer of a technological commodity. This rhetoric is misleading in that it does not ade-
quately get at the unique reliance of the platform's functioning on its base of
users. This is a fetishistic relationship that does not consider capital's ability
to make desire productive, to make it work toward the increasing con-
centration of capital. Providing us with free or cheap tools for expanding the
scope of remote communication, informational enhancement of life makes
life's subsumption under capital all the swifter and more unquestioned. This
framing fails to consider the relations of production and expropriation in the
valorization of technology. It also does not account for the unique subjection of the human user to for-profit, recursive self-styling technology.
This is overt repression of the way that psychology as a discipline is
embedded in this regime. It is one social technology among many, so its

critiques of social media should be read as a critique of a competing technology of the self, where the crucial difference between the two is that the user of psychology is a *subject* of the disciplinary institutions of modern society, whereas the user of social media is a controlled relay – not defined by its humanity, but by its existence as an account linked to other accounts that get modulated socially and technologically through this linkage.

Social production is never anything other than desiring-production. Echoing Deleuze and Guattari, I forward the notion that rather than a pathology, desire is a revolutionary agency in capitalist societies precisely because the latter deals in *interests* masquerading as desire. All the while, as they say, the capitalist axiomatic is completely incapable of accommodating desire itself. Desire is, moreover, a production of the real in itself, rather than thirst, aspiration, or a lack. It is the irrational underlying every form of rationality (1986, pp. 378–379). Accordingly, the sense in which the desiring unconscious as a living force of production is structured like a language is only that it presents the collusion between desire and the historical process of the sign's use, the sign as ever-evolving and only understandable in its situated, productive dimensions, co-emergent with the systems which it ultimately serves to model.

Deleuze and Guattari's thought elucidated a philosophy of language that aspired to go beyond the psychoanalytic theater of representation and interpretation to a materialist, immanent auto-production of the real itself. Deleuze and Guattari's formulation of the schizoanalytic unconscious is additive (rather than polemical) of the productive dimensions of subjectivity and sociality, and thus counterbalances the sense in which the subject of the unconscious is absolute negativity centered on what it is lacking. Deleuze casts off any doubt that these both equally require a bearing witness to what is constituted; a field of immanence or plane of consistency, in Guattari's (2013) later terminology. This field of immanence of substance opposes all strata of organization, *the organism's organization as well as power organization.* The enjoyment attributed to the body in the formation of the symptom in psychoanalysis, the body of theory against which they were writing, is conceived instead as real, unbridled social production that creates and recreates temporality, sexuality, and the practices of everyday life.

Desiring-production and social-production are the two faces of desire's production of the Real, as a process rather than an unreachable limit, not so much impossible to represent, but non-representational. For all its nebulous, elusive, and almost mystical veneer, it is, for all that, never natural or spontaneous, but always the result of a highly engineered montage, rich in interactions, that cannot be understood outside of a determined social apparatus. It is the result of passive syntheses, perceptual and visceral contractions that preserve and remember, that constitute the auto-production of the living force of social production that they call the un-conscious (Buchanan, 2008). Interested in the "immanent pragmatics" of the unconscious, in its machinic character, desire as a real force of pro-duction engenders the machines and functions that manufacture and express various material and immaterial flows.

Guattari (2011) describes their version of the unconscious as moving away from "affair[s] of psychological instances" to the production of en-joyment which operates "'before' objects and subjects have been specified" (p. 167). Deleuze and Guattari (1986) understand desire as a force of ab-solute production that opens the social field to what they suggest is the infinite capacity of living force. This is pressing today as far as the ex-ploitation of social production by capital is the name of the game of contemporary society and economy:

> today production is increasingly social in a double sense: on the one hand, people produce ever more socially, in networks of cooperation and interaction; and on the other, the result of production is not just commodities but social relations and ultimately society itself.
>
> *(Hardt and Negri, 2004, p. 78)*

Work is spread across a wider range of activities that are not identified as work but are presented as expressions of desire and passion, even by those who engage in them (Boltanski & Esquerre, 2016). The interwovenness of work and non-work that perpetuates our excessive use of the Internet, but is also caused by it, is a key point of indeterminacy in diagnosing Internet Addiction (i.e. whether or not one's on-line activity is considered as a piece of "real life," or against it). Capitalist modes of relation and exploitation that were developed in factory production now permeate all social relations and spaces, an idea known in autonomist Marxism as the "social factory thesis." With your smartphone in hand, you are never really off the clock, and constant access to the Internet confuses boundaries between work and lei-sure but also eats into the night; the system never sleeps, and value capture extends into every aspect of life.

The second thesis of schizoanalysis is that "within the social investments one can distinguish unconscious libidinal investments of group or desire, and the preconscious investment of class or interest (Deleuze & Guattari, 1986, p. 343–345). The economy of attention and data production, in which excessive use of the Internet plays a crucial part, must be understood in order to distinguish meaningfully between unconscious libidinal investments and investment of class-based interest. Investments of desire and investments of interest may have the same object, the socius, but different aims (namely, an aim versus a molecular phenomenon absent of a goal or an intention). The former seeks to determine itself in large social goals that take charge of the entire social organism and its collectively vested organs. The latter, libidinal investment, has no regard for regime synthesis but instead bears on the formation of power and the development of forces and energies devoid of meaning and purpose *because it is from the development of these forces from which meaning and purpose derive.*

In fact, a re-invigoration of the question of class in the informational, digital economy is a large part of what this piece attempts to address. This thesis pertains to the alien desire of/for capital, in and against libidinal investments of group or desire. It is about capital's addiction to the Internet, over and against our unconscious libidinal investments of desire. As such, it reminds us of the importance of deep discernment when it comes to analyzing or assessing the Internet use habits of ourselves and others. The entire infrastructure of modern computing and indeed of life if networks are based upon a mode of value extraction that thrives on desire's productivity, but for whom, and why? The two go even farther in their third thesis of schizoanalysis (1986, p. 356), by postulating the primacy of the libidinal investments of the social field over the familial investment, which, in their polemic against traditional psychoanalytic logic, largely equates to an investment of class or interest. Deleuze and Guattari call the great Other the nonhuman sex, that gives way, in representation, "to a signifier of the great Other as an always missing term" (1986, p. 310). Wouldn't the great Other, they ask, be the Social Other, social difference apprehended and invested as the non-family within the family itself? Here we find, in absence of analogical reasoning tying difference back to familiar (and familial) points of reference, a call for the unfettered proliferation of difference. The difference is apprehended not by analogy, making the known primary, but by the negation of *the index of what is nonhuman in sex* for which the libido assembles its desiring-machines. Contra- the psychoanalytic impetus to draw reactions of the difference back into the family in the form "X stands for Y," difference is a shock - the whole social field of desire that designates zones of intensity to which familial agents and scenes are allocated and which they populate.

For these reasons, without the context of the digital economy and the way it rearranges traditional heuristics for understanding valuable behavior, Internet Addiction is a floating signifier that may be wielded against individuals mired in the scramble the Internet creates. Seeing Internet Addiction through Deleuzo-Guattarian, critical psychological lenses means substituting "for the private subject of [desire/prohibition], split into a subject of enunciation and a subject of the statement, the collective

assemblage of enunciation of social media which refers us to machinic arrangements in which traces of data stick produced *between* users stick to and
delimit individual accounts. In a critical psychology of users, any reference
to addiction in this process may refer to (1) induction of the user into unpaid
labor through the unconscious investment of libidinal energy in the group
or in desiring-production *per se*, or (2) the production of capital or surplus
value *for-itself* that ceaselessly directs this energy into its larger system of
repression (via withholding from the commons the means of its own sub-
sistence). Even if we do away with the individualizing charges of Internet
Addiction, the question remains as to how users become hooked as a collective. While we begin to explore this question below, the rest of the piece
will describe the social formation and mechanisms of social media that make
it a social formation with formidable hooks.

Getting hooked

Desire is the productive motor of social media in a regime of cybernetic
capitalism. Social media does not exist without users and their raw material,
their abstract libido, and the proliferation of difference per se. And yet, the
lives increasingly mired in "liking," "sharing," button-pushing, and other
exercises of the use and administration of social technologies of self modulation have no financial share in the massive wealth of collective memory
to which they contribute. They have instead, in addition to the substantial
psychical reconfigurations of social media, the reproduction of social networks of care. This implies and has borne out a veritable explosion of
subcultures, special interest groups, radical networks of artists and activists.
The fact of collective, online migration pays its user *in kind* for the act of
social reproduction at ground zero.

   The phenomenon of increased screen time turns out to also be a generalized and very real, *migration to online platforms*. On social media, the fact
of giving time and attention to the platform and the remote others with
whom users become connected is also a veritable capture of such activity in
accordance with the commercial and capital requirements of the platform.
Bruce Alexander's (2008) "dislocation theory of addiction" comes closest to
this formulation in tying the etiology of addiction to the struggle over
landed space and territories. The dislocation theory posits that addictions are
born primarily of mass migrations of laborers in the wake of imperial colonization by way of global Northern hegemony. While developments in
telecommunications correspond to advances in international transportation
and migration, the possibilities for instant interaction across dispersed

communities offer visions of life no longer constrained by territorially bounded nation-states (Kleiner, 2010).

Capitalism has always created "dislocation" by engineering rapid cultural change and "disadjustments" between technological systems and the social support systems in place to ensure the integration of society's members. Because of the global nature of capitalism that jumps from one hot spot of manufacture to another, proletarians migrate. They move where capital needs them, or autonomously to escape misery and exploitation brought on by these processes in their places of origin. Social media makes it easier for geographically dispersed networks of care to stay in touch, seek out greener pastures, and find work, even as they become tools for surveillance and vetting for potential bosses. The effect of this dislocation is nevertheless to make us all proletarianized in the form of ultra-adaptability, and an ever-burning and churning regime of fashioning and re-fashioning with new semiotic elements. This parallels the way that business and marketing practices are also today obsessively focused on novelty and innovation, fostering brief but intense commitments and enthusiasm for life that rests on a vision of human beings as flexible, versatile, and youthfully absorbent (Boltanski & Chiapello, 2005).

Mobile devices, the primary access points to the interfaces of social media, molds to the exigencies of life created by macro-social conditions live poverty and precarity, all the while maintaining them as such (Dyer-Witheford, 2015). While a global labor force produces the devices we use to access social media, social media and the devices needed to access it are also a means of finding temporary work and "gigs." Without these technologies, the spread of low-waged, informal work engaged by the often unwittingly self-employed would be impossible to manage. This applies as much to the developing world as it does to North America. The inclusion of mobile-enabled social media use can be considered a component of a new phase of capitalist subsumption characterized by the digitization of everything, across the plant. In the context of labor, it enables and disables connection to pools of disposed laborers, dispossessed by capital's processes of globalization. Facebook and other social media software are often rightfully understood as a strange ensemble of self-performances.

Social media is inevitably utilized by a precarious, nomadic workforce made so by the adjustments forwarded by the insights and globalizing processes afforded by digital technologies. Beyond bringing us online as social media users, digitization has been a boon to globalized production processes by introducing integrated supply chains, high-tech agribusiness, and high-frequency trading. These developments displace human bodies, driving migration to urban areas and to increased screen time; schematically speaking, in the global South they give rise to screen time that mitigates the pain of physical distance, whereas, in wealthier countries from which much agricultural and industrial production has fled, micro-labor, gig work, and all stripes of managerial jobs are operated through smartphones and laptops.

Our hypothesis vis-a-vis a collective notion of Internet Addiction is that, in a time when the leading edge of production occurs through the perpetual mass migration of laborers and digital commodities in and through fiber optic cables connecting the whole globe, addiction is ubiquitous because, in a very particular sense, we are *all migrants and nomads, all the time*. With respect to the imperialism of digital technologies, Deleuze and Guattari's general rule, which takes a Marxian tone beyond Marx, applies. Primitive accumulation occurs upon the mounting of an apparatus of capture, with a kind of violence that is particular: it creates or contributes to the creation of that which it is directed against, and thus presupposes itself (1987, p.447). What is created is a humanity-wide marketplace, and the sad affects of addiction – loss of control, compulsion, *is the very pathos of entrance into this market*. What it means that people and psyches are marketized, with the pathic description of subjection to capitalism and its creation of a labor market, simply doesn't read. It doesn't even begin to touch the space within which one is made one, within which one broaches the farcical nature of the ideologies of freedom, and of consent. It is perfect repetition of a primordial stolenness of choice that I suggest here is a unique form of coercive mass migration. On social media, we also try to *release* the sad affects of rivalry, hatred, loss, and envy to the social media machine that creates and exacerbates them. We imagine some agency digests all of it, when in fact, much of this fodder simply comes back to haunt us and, of course, to sell us things.

Knowledge of the ambient state and corporate surveillance on social media platforms has exploded in the last few years, and yet there has been almost no chance in the rate of growth of Facebook users (Dutton et al., 2013). We know that we were emotionally manipulated in a series of unapproved studies performed by Facebook itself (Kramer et al., 2014). We know that Facebook is scraped by artificial intelligence companies that report to police and federal agents. We know that Facebook takes no responsibility for the spread of hate speech (Levin, 2018). We know that Facebook's hacks have contributed to the manipulation of national elections. We know, and yet we continue to be there. We know very well what is happening, and we stay there all the same. Why? We are enslaved by capitalist social machinery. How is it so coercive as to effect a total social capture? It preys upon those who are reliant upon it for an opportunity, and brings everyone else with it in the process, either because they are hungry for opportunity or because they know somebody who is. Tangential from but related to this hunger is the hunger for presence, resulting from the atomization and isolation of the current dominant regime of work best described as the precarious but also affected by the neoliberalization of the economy and the de- and re-proletarianization to which we are submitted.

In Thoburn's *Deleuze, Marx, and Politics* (2003), there are three inter-related aspects of Deleuze and Guattari's minor politics that help frame an expansive reading of Marx's category of the proletariat. Reviewing them here will enable us to understand the condition of the user from a historical perspective, which is especially important considering the compulsion to engage in this high-stakes capitalist game without being paid or employed in the traditional sense. The first aspect of minor politics related to the pro-letariat is a politics *against identity*. The second is an emphasis on social relations and the third an intensive mode of engagement. These three as-pects come sharply into view on social media, as a part of its architecture and its facticity, rather than as properties of a particular kind of excessive or intensive use. Here the heuristic of "major" or "minor" politics becomes a question of how different groups, movements, and concerns related to the dominant regime of signs. Simply put, it helps determine major and minor uses of digital technologies. Deleuze and Guattari expressed this distinction also in their fourth thesis of schizoanalysis.

This fourth thesis postulates the distinction between two poles of social libidinal investment: the paranoiac, reactionary, and fascizing pole, and the schizoid revolutionary pole (1986, p. 366). The two poles are defined, one, by the enslavement of production and the desiring-machines to the gre-garious aggregates that they constitute on a large scale under a given form of power or selective sovereignty; the other by the inverse subordination and overthrow of power (*ibid*, p. 366). The oscillation between the two poles is a constituent aspect of the delirium of the social media assemblage. The two poles do not maintain the same relationship, nor the same form of re-lationship, with the preconscious investments of interest. This thesis pertains to resistance and counter-resistance to net-related crises. Another way to think of this is that there are both vertical and horizontal social relations that condition our dependence on the value produced by the Internet. On the one hand, vertical relations of ownership carry forward massive power asymmetries typical of contemporary capitalism that profit from the con-tinuing destabilization and global scramble of bodies that creates both the very cheap "workforce" of data-producing users, and on the other hand the horizontal relations of identification we have with each other, between users, that creates a profound willingness to participate in these technological networks.

The poles of the fascizing reactionary and the schizoid revolutionary sets the stage for the sorts of struggles and contradictions that compose the overlapping matrices of the digitally interconnected world. It is quite significant that the pair created a continuum of reactionary fascism and schizoid revolution on opposite sides, subtly dismissing the possibility of revolutionary fascism and implicitly reserving revolution for disperse, quickly moving, and perhaps even aimless forces of desire. This also the highly anti- or simply non-statist bent of schizoanalysis, in which a non-identitarian politics of desire is more closely related to economic than political forces. The poles of libidinal investment help us tell a story of the gerrymandering of inscription, agency, and alliance between and across human users and corporate platforms, with legislative bodies and political elites in a relatively minor role. Nevertheless, the digital social body is incessantly re-volutionizing desire as concerns intra- and inter-personal relationships that amplify and display their importance against their increasing inter-mediation by intelligent machines and the physical distancing of actual human bodies.

What follows explores the connection of users to the social media platform, and in turn, to the capitalist axiomatic online. We will see, nevertheless, that user participation is not "work" in the traditional sense. There is instead evidence of the compulsion to engage in the reproduction of social relations for their own sake, to the degree that psychologists point out indeed competes directly with the supposed interests of well-functioning individuals. The compulsion or dependence in play here attests to the force of a collective migration beneath and beyond individual choice. For sociologist Alex Foti (2017), the *precariat* (as opposed to the proletariat) is an internally divided class-in-the-making that consists of a "multitude" of insecure denizens with a limited range of social, cultural, political, and economic opportunities. They live bits and pieces of lives, moving in and out of short-term jobs. Just like the time-sink diagnosis of Internet Addiction, the precariat is theorized as having no control over its time or its economic security. This insecurity chips away at altruism, tolerance, reciprocity, and social solidarity, and social media rebuilds the necessary minimum of these for the reproduction of the precarious class. In contrast to the proletariat of the industrial age, the precariat's relations of production are defined through partial involvement in labor and lots of "work-for-labor" like the sort of self-advertisement that goes on social media. They are opportunistic precisely for lack of belonging to professional and craft communities, and for social memory or shadow of the future hanging over their deliberations, and risk being lured in by neo-fascists in the US, Sweden, Finland, France, Japan, and Great Britain. As in the existing fascism of interwar Europe, social instability portrayed below as the mediatic social management of transient desire opens the door for militant ideologies and propagandists to proclaim a return to order and to simpler times of lesser exposure to any "outside."

As we have said, social media does also serve the function of maintaining (largely pre-existing) networks of care, reciprocity, and duty. The upsurge in mutual care efforts owes in part to the utility of social media for circulating scarce resources, like money and household goods. Non-users or those who hope to quit face an even deeper social isolation than when they were using. The participatory nature of Facebook hails us as global, self-consistent people who want to be "in relation." This takes on the well-known form of the "fear of missing out," where the fear of missing out is not an insignificant form of weakness, but what I consider a sign of collective migration. Collective migration hinges on social inclusion and by extension, survival. This takes the form of preservation, as when one claims to want to keep in touch with people and opportunities that have already migrated there, and discovery, typified in new manifestations of the abstract desire for a category of other, as in possible colleagues on LinkedIn, possible dates on Tinder, and possible political allies on Twitter. As we know, it is often a mandate, as in the neoliberal university's use of third party software or when academia.edu creates a profile for you without your having ever signed up and refusing to accede makes finding the next non-tenure-track position difficult.

The most interesting part of migration into digital space as an alternative or a supplement is that, when it is considered in its entirety to include all users, it is by necessity less tightly coupled to histories or migrations from *here* to *there*, with their clearly delineated indigenous, national, and religious identities. Is there an opening here for a politics of desire, beyond identity? Which is to say, for the "use" of the schizoid revolutionary pole of desiring-production as opposed to the galvanizing force of the paranoid, reactionary pole? There is no shared base of rituals or relations to which we may collectively hope to return – only a shared subjection, as raw material, for the production of speculative value, indifferent to the particulars of what is created (or re-created) in digital space. In other words, we need not assimilate, but we must *be* there. If the interior edge of the capitalist semiotic is the usurping of archaisms, traditions, and stratifications borrowed from older systems, the culture machine of social media exemplifies how a wide variety of "unresolved" archaisms come to populate the space as its raw material (by way of the user and its proclivities, unconscious tendencies, and unchecked assumptions).

4
USERS AND TECHNOLOGIES OF SELF

Regimes of signs and subjectivity

The global collectivity of users subjectivated by the United States' social media machines and their uptake around the world are ignored by Psychology or referred to in a piecemeal and extreme way by the diagnostic category, Internet Addiction. The addict of psychology, coinciding with its understanding of the brain and learning for all human beings, is marked by a strong form of flexibility and gregariousness of desire correlative to desire's direct productivity in the real subsumption of society by capital. The following study of the assemblage of social media and its users points to a common fabric of subjectification on and through the Internet. This is not without its opportunities for ethics and aesthetics of self. However, these are linked with and situated amidst the precarizing de- and re-territorialization of bodies, labor, and capital assisted by aggregate masses of user data and their analysis. This includes social media companies' own enslavement to the needs of capital by way of private property and private persons, which is made more ironic given the way its tools demonstrate pre- and trans-personal becoming. Through centralized mediation of peer-to-peer networks, implacable and enigmatic flows of desire are re-coded, homogenized, and twisted toward the mandates of capital for its own sake, with an underclass of dependent users as a byproduct.

One of Guattari's many definitions of subjectivity is "the ensemble of conditions which render possible the emergence of individual and/or collective instances as self-referential existential Territories, adjacent, or in a delimiting relation, to alterity that is itself subjective" (Guattari, 1995, p. 9). Guattari's (1984, 1995, 2008, 2013, 2015) frenetic body of solo-authored work spanned many pages predicting future deployments of various technologies that both analyze and *produce* subjectivity. Beyond individualization and identitarian foreclosures of the other and of the new, he perceived collective and individual subjectivity as open on all sides to socius, to techno-scientific universes of reference, to aesthetics, and also to pre- and trans-personal understandings of time, the body, and sexuality.

Guattari's interest was in tracing the developments that transform linguistics, from the territorialized (phonological) sign of tribal economies to the semantic and syntactic signs of the relatively deterritorialized state and its divisions of labor to an increasingly pragmatic a-signifying sign in the hyper-deterritorialized present (Deleuze, 1995, p. 28). In the progression of linguistics, Guattari found a phylogenetic relationship to the historical deterritorialization of the sign, the contemporary pinnacle of which is the register-crossing, multi-use semiotic register of *data*. Collective apparatuses of subjectification correspond to this diachronic progression in an important way; they allow us to grasp these apparatuses as they are layered on each other, always added rather than replacing, as history roils on. There is always an imbrication and contemporaneity of modes of inscription, or what Guattari called "voices" in *Schizoanalytic Cartographies* (2013). Pathic subjectivity is not only subject to language but manufactured by what he calls voices/pathways to which it responds (taking advantage of the French voie/voix to denote the path dependencies of the machinic, organizational unconscious). As we will see, these general techniques of the inscription of bodies owe to and connect with dominant forms of oppression and subjugation.

Guattari understood the most fundamental subjective mutations as functions of the birth of collective religious/cultural apparatuses, on the one hand, and the invention of new materials, energies, machines that crystallize time, and biotechnologies, on the other. While material infrastructures do not condition collective subjectivity directly, we can map components that are essential to the taking of consistency of different voices/pathways in space and time as a function of technical, scientific, and artistic transformation. Taking for granted that informatic and communicational machines contribute to and prepare assemblages of enunciation, Guattari names three series of voices or pathways that function as collective apparatuses of subjectification in contemporary Western societies but whose presence or indirect effects are increasingly felt all over the globe. These series are voices/pathways of power, knowledge, and self-reference. While self-reference is the dominant voice today, it is shot through with, and in a sense, formulated from, the first two voices in the assemblage that is social media. These voices collide in a strange dance that readily prompts new figures forged from archaisms, specifically their combinations, intersections, and encounters with alterity.

The first voice, of power, is exemplary in relation to the Age of European Christianity that succeeded the Roman and Carolingian Empires. Relating the Earth and power in a new way, human groups are seized by imaginary holds of flexible monotheism which erect a disciplinary grid that circumscribes or circumvents human groups from the outside, by direct coercion and panoptic hold on bodies. In a regime of territorialized signs, subjectivity is doubly articulated to the Feudal segmentarity of existentially autonomous entities of national, religious, and ethnic texture and the de-territorialized entity of subjective power inhering in the flexible mono-theism as a collective apparatus across autonomous segmentations. Its signs are territorialized, and its consistency factors come together to actualize territorialized series, even in the face of wars and epidemics.

The second voice, of knowledge, involves deterritorialized semiotics marked by a general equivalence of abstract power from the flattening of different modes of valorization. Where territorialized assemblages of enunciation are tethered to the subjects and objects of speech and direct communication, deterritorialized assemblages of enunciation do not pre-suppose particular material instantiations. Symbolic capitalization steps in for a despot or God that once served to cement existential territories. This is where the principle of generalized equivalence, articulated from within subjectivity to technoscientific and economic pragmatics that endure on the basis of temporal reformulations that race ahead of, and thus relaunch, its stakes to deterritorialized social classes. Printed text that archived and han-dled knowledge in broader stead than oral performance, deployments of steam and steel that launch machinic vectors through the increasingly visible division of urban and non-urban spaces, chronometry and monetary credit's effects on rhythms and temporality, and the bio-taxonomical revolution all speak in this voice (Guattari, 2013).

As the most singular, contingent, and finite of these voices/pathways, self-reference is also the most universal. However, Guattari quickly clarified that it is not universal in a strict sense, but the richest in *Universes of virtuality*, or the best furnished with lines of processuality. This important clarification implies that the dominance of the voice of self-reference also creates a wealth of possibilities for the creation of new social forms. Through the rest of this book, we look at the precise mechanisms through which self-reference affords the opportunity for the perfusion of signifiers, linguistic and non-linguistic, through the reticular structure of social media, albeit in the fraught "house" of corporate social media servers. We can say that when it comes to the voice of self-reference, the primary purpose of semiotic series is not to denote states of facts or organize states of sense along axes of signification, but to crystallize existential posits that manage to align with the principles of classical reason (Guattari, 2013).

The difficulty in bringing out exactly how these function is that the materials used for these existential crystallizations are extracted from radically heterogeneous elements, like the rhythms of life and lived experience, across multiple, competing temporalities. They come just as well from obsessive refrains, cobbled together from the conjoined threats of the inhuman within the human (as in the trope of addictive lures that beckon to the feeding beasts within) and the human within the inhuman (as in the equation of the human and the nonhuman in the expansive category of the user) that haunt the contemporary understanding of digital subjectivity. Indeed, self-reference has a profound ability to foment possessive, and self-possessive, individualism.

Self-reference also refers to machinic and automated feedback loops, such that primary mechanisms of social power are the ability to refer to and amplify the self- or entity-sustaining functions. Cybernetic reflexivity is therefore also how creativity and acts of resistance online are captured as surplus value for social media platforms (Dean, 2010, 2013). It is this repetitive movement of machine processing that creates this highly unevenly distributed surplus value. The perpetual construction and reconstruction of a self, an ongoing diagram or working model, can be liberatory and inventive or can snowball into crippling anxiety. Taking not the self, but the private person, the self-image as its object, a hysterical dialectic that takes the "self-image," be it of an individual, a social group, an institution, or a nation-state, as an object, becomes available.

Another facet of Bateson's (2000) account of addictions points out that the fundamental fantasy of alcoholism, as a proxy for all other addictions, is a global self-capable of either total control over, or total submission to, drinking. This justifies his explanation of twelve-step groups as a specific use, or technology, of self. Such a technology sustains a notion of individuality that presupposes control over their lives and in the value of their assigned place in society. In the moment of subjection, this higher unity constitutes the human being as the subject, linked to an exteriorized object. It assumes the tenets of legal personhood associated with Western, liberal political subjects. Bateson's (1990) model of the relationship between the alcoholic and the imagined other is instructive: This dialectic consists of offering one's activity in service of a self-image and refusing to do so. One can always exploit, cast off, or amplify an identitarian fragment with torrential streams of rationalizing fodder available online. Too often, desire is aided by thought that moves quickly enough only to enables brief, binary bursts of paranoiac closure that fade, requiring plenty of active participation in order to be revived and reestablished in mediatic loops.

A regime of cybernetic self-reflexivity as applied to the user points to an explosion of means by which to see, know, and therefore to modulate, itself. Where repression and molding in disciplinary social institutions sought to limit peculiarities so that individuals could recognize themselves through a series of limited distinctions (think demographic coordinates, or sizes S, M, and L, for example), excesses of data pertaining to users and their accounts afford a nuanced personalization of goods, services, media, and suggestions until, eventually, every user has a completely unique version of everything and users are buried in themselves and their formative relations. Already we see hints of how this also entails the voices of power as segmented identitarian forces that are spun out, tested in a play of general equivalence (the voice of knowledge), and that "touch the ground" as seen in affordances of access, privileges, red tape and restrictions vis-a-vis social institutions and digitally-mediated physical spaces.

For the purposes of this analysis, we can interpret Guattari's claims about the voice of self-reference as a directive to not only take a critical perspective on the pathological kind, Internet Addiction but also to understand users as a collective social body with the potential to transform itself through a new movement of thought (Simondon, 2014). The rise of self-reference, commonly critiqued in the framework of individual utterances to indicate a rise in mass narcissism, also indicates that whole social groups have the means to self-correct rather than remaining first-order observers. Self-reference was Guattari's theorization of reflexivity or a mode of understanding reflexivity that is neither indebted to a techno-utopian vision of participatory, flexible, and homeostatic self-regulating systems, nor to Ulrich Beck's "risk society" (though it does index these). The techniques of this reflexivity of self (again, of any ontological entity, not necessarily a human being) will frame how we understand social media, with its interfaces, algorithms, and users.

This dynamic struggle between, on the one hand, "network being," with its collective nature and exciting potentials, and a profit-motivated insistence on the enculturated maintenance of the individual subject, on the other, is born out in the excessive (and mundane) use of social media. Lazzarato (2014) follows Deleuze and Guattari, in proclaiming that today's production of subjectivity is located between social subjection and machinic enslavement. From a semiotic perspective, machinic enslavement and social subjection entail distinct regimes of signs. Social subjection mobilizes signifying semiotics, the voice of knowledge especially, aimed at consciousness, and mobilizes representations with a view to constituting an individual subject. On the other hand, machinic enslavement functions based on a-signifying semiotics of computational self-reflexivity, like stock market indices, currency, mathematical equations, diagrams, computer languages, national and corporate accounting, etc., which do not involve consciousness and representations and do not have the subject as referent (Lazzarato, 2014 p. 39). Machinic enslavement blends the voices of power, and its direct inscription, with the self-reference of complex systems.

Guattari's posthumously published "Capital as the integral of power formations" pits machinic enslavement against the notion of the "subjugation of the masses in terms of ideological deceit or a collective masochistic passion," claiming that machinic enslavement seizes individuals from the inside rather than through the grips of some social identity or persona through which subjectification (of the Althusserian kind) was said to take hold (1996, p. 261). Machinic enslavement is how capitalism settles into the hearts of individuals, how it comes to directly involve functions of perception, affects, and unconscious behaviors and grafts them onto capitalist machinery. Importantly, he notes that this taking "possession of labor-power and desire ... extends far beyond that of the working class, sociologically speaking" meaning that class relations "tend to evolve differently. They are less polarized and increasingly rely on complex strategies" (*ibid*, p. 262–263). For Guattari, the machine and machinic enslavement belong to the essence of human desire, combining infrapersonal and infrasocial elements that cannot be contained by the stratified social relationships of subjugation.

Machinic enslavement is used in several ways in Deleuze and Guattari's writings and was taken up with the greatest vigor by the Italian autonomist Marxists to describe the machinations of digital capitalism. Yet, at the time of those writings, digital technologies were just barely beginning to come into popular awareness. They were deeply prophetic, delineating concepts that would become strikingly applicable and manifestly useful for the forthcoming mass adoption that would take "machinic enslavement" to the hilt, playing it off social subjection in sophisticated ways. Now, the representational nature of speech is progressively over- and under-determined by the collection and processing of ambient, actionable data, thanks to the digital technologies we encounter everywhere. Being online constitutes "us" as a mass of "dividuals," or as lump sums of human activity out of which the individual unconscious is posited. Machinic enslavement refers to this integration of human, tool, and animal into a higher unity, whether by a despotic state or in automation by and through the capital. Social subjection, on the other hand, preserves the isolation of the human from the machine such that the individual being itself becomes the higher unity — a worker, a user, etc., that is subjected to the machine rather than enslaved as a part of it (Deleuze & Guattari, 1987, p. 457). We are either abstract subjective capacity, or the specific bearer or rights and responsibilities, and these two modes of social power are shown here to be tactfully played against each other.

The way that identities function online is part of the machinery (in addition to psychology's aforementioned privation of the brain) of the reproduction of private persons. Deleuze and Guattari would call them simulacra (images of images) that have an aptitude for representing the first-order images of social persons. Especially when viewing social media from this perspective, there exists the opportunity to see the fracture between the subject of enunciation, the speaker, and the subject of the statement, the spoken, as a requirement of the axiomatic of capital in its deterritorializing (becoming-abstract, becoming-multiple) and reterritorializing (fixed quantities of rigid, unmistakable origins) movements. The capitalist axiomatic operates through abstraction and quantification of productive forces, constituting machinic enslavement from which it produces molar aggregates. These aggregates, the worker, the businessperson, the entrepreneur are social subjections. Social subjections are human embodiments of the various effects of capitalist dynamics. Online, this process begins with the aggregate of the social group which is then dissolved through abstraction and quantification as a pool of data. From this pool of data emerges the reconstruction of individuals whose particular characteristics are reified and refined out of this pool of data. Users are quantized and "dividualized" only to become even more vivid and speculative images of their "real" personhood.

This conception of subjectivity and capture hearkens back to the pair's critique of Freud. In *Anti-Oedipus* they charge him with making the "profound discovery of the abstract subjective essence of desire, libido" but then "re-alienating this essence, reinvesting it in a subjective system of representation of the ego" which they refer to as the territoriality of Oedipus (1986, p. 333). The discovery of the abstract subjective essence of desire is the same as the discovery of the decoded and deterritorialized flows of subjective abstract labor that takes place in social production and political economy (*ibid*, p. 302). The secret sauce of both capitalism and traditional psychoanalysis from which much current psychological practice derives today is the activity of production in general and without distinction. The greater intensity of capitalist appropriation and extraction makes use of this discovery by turning repression and prohibition on its head and aggressively provoking the free flow of desire, as to hone and control it. This historical phenomenon has been called a shift to "societies of control" (Deleuze, 1992), "societies of enjoyment" (McGowan, 2012), or the "achievement society" (Han & DeMarco, 2018).

For this reason, schizoanalysis proposes a reversal of the Freudian topology where the unconscious and the series of drives together called the "id" does not apply pressure to consciousness, the "ego," but vice versa. Consciousness puts a stranglehold on the unconscious to prevent its escape. Because libido is the energy and the transformation of the energy of desiring-machines, it is the unconscious investment of libido that directly invests the large aggregates of the social and organic fields. Insofar as these connections form free, molecular multiplicities, unfettered by molar representations, schizoanalysis seeks to identify and analyze the "n-sexes" of the non-anthropomorphized subject and to ask what use is made of them as they extend from the molecular to the molar (pp. 290–296). A historical, collective, "schizoanalysis" looks at the processual dynamics of the social media machine as a collective assemblage of enunciation that articulates humans together with digital technologies to show how these assemblages individualize users from a constitutive global, collectivity of users not conscious of their collective power. Such users have migrated online, but also across borders, and into and out of informal, often economic, networks that further enmesh and invest them socially in digital networks.

For the dividual, in contrast to the individual that the psy-disciplines and social media seek to reinstate, desire and libido are specifically unleashed as an overwhelming excess. This excess is concomitant with a turning away from the individual; all that matters is the population-level modulation of "dividuals" composed of individuals with all sorts of bizarre traits, habits, tastes, and aptitudes formerly repressed in the molding of individuals in the disciplinary society of time passed. Users of digital services like social media exemplify this process. In an excessive use of digital technologies, the subjective unconscious becomes transparent to the user as a series of optional matters in the commodity production of the self, online, subject to excesses of communication, and temporality of hyper-immediacy.

Users are a category of agents created by digital systems and their redistribution of agency. Outside of these systems of information flow and exchange, users have no essential role or identity. This makes it possible for the position of the user to be filled by an animal, an artificial intelligence (a bot), or some other machine. Note that the position of users within this system does not represent a mastery or convergence of other layers of digital information flow, though it is the sole locus where the effects of this flow are gathered into a figure or persona whom it is easy to recognize as a person (Bratton, 2015). The position of users is therefore not positively qualified according to the vectors of subjection (citizenship, social status, familial relations), but is defined instead by that to which it connects. This is how the agency is already constructed in advance by affordances of *access*, and what makes Bratton (2015) write, in his excellent account of the user position, that any notion of user sovereignty more likely draws, not from established rights *per se*, but from the slippage between access granted to citizens as distinct from pre-established, generic user privileges on a particular platform.

Users and technologies of self

Digital social media are designed to highlight and even to verify users as individual atomic unities. Familiarly, it is the human individual toward whom the mouse and keyboard were geared, and at whom biological, behavioral, and other identificatory markers are offered as useful means of tracking. The user encapsulates and drives to the hilt vectors of social subjection. In a regime of self-reflexivity, the perspective of the outside observer is internalized, and possibilities for identification, different ways-to-be, become ideal targets of self-modulation. This process of the marketization of human users (as attention-givers to digital content and advertisements) creates an unprecedented degree of exposure to other users and other possible users, like bots, machines, and nonhuman actors. Being unique, it turns out, has little to do with liberty or dignity on its own. Instead, as Guattari (1989, p. 50) writes in *Three Ecologies,* capitalistic subjectivity gains ground by "controlling and neutralizing the maximum number of existential refrains." Not only are users made interchangeable and comparable through technologies of quantitative self-reflection, but the position of the user is also granted to nonhuman agents, making this reduction of subjectivity patently obvious to users who regularly encounter this fact.

This interplay between the dividual and the individual means that the social subject does not go away but takes on a new role in the assemblage of digital subjectivity. We turn now to look at the repetition of social subjection in this interplay through the lens of Focault's (1988) historical study of the technologies of the self. "Technologies of the Self" is a question that appeared at the end of the 18th century, which was to become one of the poles of modern philosophy. Through studying madness and psychiatry, crime and punishment, Foucault showed how we constitute ourselves indirectly, through the exclusion of others (criminals, mad people, etc.). At the time of his writing, post-World War II institutions like welfare, public health, and medical assistance programs demonstrated how the care for individual life became a duty for the state.

Statistics and its requisite data collection rose to prominence for its ability to reveal something about the status of populations, and therefore knowledge of different states' respective degrees of force. The logic behind statistical techniques performed on population data as a measure of the state's degree of force relies on the integration of individuals in the state's utility on the margins. The government is worried about individuals, on this account, as far as he or she can influence the strength of the state either positively or negatively. As Foucault (1988, p. 152) states candidly, "sometimes what he has to do for the state is to live, to work, to produce, to consume; and sometimes what he has to do is die." The integration of individuals is obtained by *policing*. In many ways, social media accounts for the ways that individuals have been made to police each other, as unpaid work that states outsource to corporations, that corporations outsource to us, even as we are the objects of this policing.

Foucault sought the techniques and practices that correspond to this political rationality and to the new kind of relationship between the social entity and the individual. The integration of the individual in a totality results from a constant correlation between hyper-individualization and hyper-reinforcement of this totality. The individual is integrated into society, in large part, by social media as a sort of final bastion of sociality for those who are inside of but also on the margins of the "disciplinary" social institutions like the school, the prison, the asylum, and so on. In the origins of policing as examined by Foucault, the meaning of policing was the techniques by which individual people could be governed as significantly useful for the world. Everything a person does or undertakes, all of the conditions that comprise their being, their relations to others, to things, and to nature become the object of policing. Policing deals with all influences on the happiness of humans, which again is now an element of state strength. It therefore also deals with society, the relations of which it is composed, and really, with life itself.

Foucault's analysis of technologies of self-sketches a history of the ways in our culture that people develop knowledge about themselves, what he calls "truth games" of self-understanding. Social media is undoubtedly a profound, secular addition to this history. They reiterate his notion of governmentality and Deleuze's (1992, 1995) notion of control: the contact between the technology of domination and technologies of the self. Stoic "technologies of self" included acts like writing letters to friends in which one disclosed the activities and attitudes of the self, privately examining the self and the conscience, and reviewing what was done compared to what should have been done. Memory serves this goal in that statements remembered were to become subjectivized rules for conduct and mastery. This occurred not through renunciation of self, but the subjective assimilation and acquisition of the truth of teachers, the incorporation of which implied greater access to reality. The practice of interpreting dreams was, in this era, nascent and marginal at best.

The conditions of absolute surveillance by algorithmic omniscience, its science of social organization, and the mass audience to which it gives rise are reminiscent of confessional technology, which Foucault analyzes from early to modern Christianity. On the healing model "one must see it to change it," the general air of privation of self-technologies of the Stoics was replaced with a highly public confessional in which the sinner proved suffering, showed shame, made humility visible, and put newfound modesty on display. The truth of oneself had to be recognized, disclosed to God, and to those in the community. Public confession before God and man created the conditions for people to become hermeneuts of themselves, speaking and transcribing as many thoughts as possible. In this paradigm, expression of thought would, ideally, be ongoing. Now it is. The human sciences are quite obviously a part of this too, as they expressly aim to create new selves out of its subjects. This is how psychology and social media can be conceived together, as competing, contemporary technologies of the self.

Vis-a-vis the social relations fostered by the social platform, Facebook, Stiegler (2013) addresses two processes. One is the ongoing creation of a profile, which amounts to a self-description by way of one's relations, and the other, a dialogue which constitutes a process of socialization. He focuses on writing as a mnemotechnic, shared across humans, for formalizing relationships:

> The self-profiling function could of course be an exercise in reflexivity for the person practicing it, but it has as principal effect to bring the new member of this type of network to declare his or her social belonging as if he or she were an ethnographer, and to thereby engage, if not in auto-ethnography, then at least in an auto-sociography by declaring and writing his or her network attachments – especially concerning friendships, but also interests of all kinds, including the most trivial and venal ones (p. 22).

As with other social processes of writing that intensify and make explicit social relations, documentation and archiving create a psychic intensification of what is already the case or of what one hopes to bring about in the act itself. Such archival documentation has the capacity to intensify bonds by making public affirmations of them, which has a range of effects: they are made firm from within, visible from the outside, and the affirmation also initiates computational processes that increase mutual self-exposure. The enormous multiplication of relations confined within one digital platform can have a flattening or chilling effect, where mindfulness of the congealing of many different offline social contexts appeals to the lowest common denominator: everyone, and so, therefore, no one. Yet, beneath the will for these efforts and the self-image that may or may not be involved in this willingness is a map of living social relations that may in fact testify to surprising attachments, proclivities, desires, and concerns.

Consider the timeline. By tracking events and enriching this tracking with stories built from other timelines, the homogeneity of human existence becomes apparent. Aggregating information behind the scenes from a host of data collection agencies across the Internet duplicates this self-reflection by scaffolding an eerie feeling of being known. When one has the sense that they are entirely predictable in advance, built from their past selves meant to progress linearly with new consumer "innovations," the options one has are either to settle into a decaying or pre-figured self-image "the you you are given," or to use the available tools in the marketplace of abstract personhood to seek out yet new "ways-to-be" options and ramping up self-tracking and tracking of external variables needed to afford satisfactory "tastes" of these options. This is where the Deleuzo-Guattarian notion of affect as a process of existential appropriation becomes a socio–economic category.

As if to skew the securing of self via avowal to the other, users' posts, status updates, and stories provide neither clarity nor guarantee about who or what attends such avowals. Presupposing their automatic archiving, we inform and demand of no one in particular – the abstract "All" of our lives, but also, in default settings mode, to the entirety of the Internet (insofar as we, in turn, are searchable by our proper names). This is the circuit of attachment and dependence forged between the personalized instantiations of the computational universe and users on the platform. Access to a world of alterity that lacks programmed moments of closure or stopping points, think "infinite scroll," creates the drive for expressive and affirmative selfhood because self, too, is never a being, but a processual becoming. In its profound capacity both to facilitate encounters with image-based, textual, and auditory alterity, and to fortify narcissistic semblances that cover over them, the on-line experience is overtaking or overwhelming precisely insofar as objects and habits of enjoyment appear as a series of disruptions heralding the "next thing" which demands users' attention.

The seeking that takes place on Facebook, and its algorithmic over-determination, embodies the epistemology of solutions on which the platform is founded. In Foucault's (1988) genealogy of technologies of the self, he pointed to an inversion: Where for the Greeks knowledge of oneself was an outcome of the care of the self, knowledge of the self was in early Christianity and through modernity a fundamental principle conditioning access to any knowledge whatsoever. This is a combined product of the secular tradition of external, social basis for morality (law) and Christian morality of asceticism which suggests that the self is that which one can reject. The place of authoritative consistency governing these operations is the platform's algorithmic knowledge which holds also the consistency of the social totality as to be able to make dependable suggestions about the "next new thing." The platform's algorithmic knowledge and its linkage with a sweeping body of folk knowledge that is always being written support an ominous sense of asymmetrical knowledge/power whereby users are given over to the truth of the incompleteness or unsatisfactory nature of knowledge – even if being on the platform tests this over and over again.

One can only send signs, intended for someone, somewhere out there. Who, or what, answers, and from where do the responses of our appeals come? The recipient of our signs is often a matter of fate and chance, and the sheer volume of Facebook use attests to an enacted belief that our social relations are interchangeable and subject to metaphoric substitution. How else could the All be an actionable addressee of language? We lose concern for our addressee, whose place is taken by this general social body. The "out-there" is constructed based on actual networks of users and the imagination engaging in it provokes across users. Identifications become more specific when one uses Facebook's group pages, where users communicate under the banner of special interests or preexisting affiliations. Such groups are nevertheless anchoring domains or landing pads for subjects located in the interchangeability of the All of an algorithmically personalized social totality.

Rather than bring to light repressed or unknown information about the subject or provide tools for understanding the contents of the platform in their context or sequence, social media simply *creates* more and more recordable information through a massive succession of disembodied encounters. Guattari's solo writings consistently remark on the wide variety of objects that contribute to existential production — usually in the form of a lament of the limits of the Freudian and Lacanian objects of focus, like the breast, faces, genitals, etc. As per the schizoanalytic contention, that desire invests the entirety of the social field without circumscription by familial relations, he emphasized the "partial subjectivity" initiated by elements that elude self-mastery, like "the repetitive symptom, the prayer, the ritual of the "session," the order word, the emblem, the refrain, the faciliatary crystallization of the celebrity" and institutional objects that could be "architectural, economic, or Cosmic" (2008, p. 56).

So, heeding the schizoanalytic call to examine the functioning of "one's own desiring machines," the first positive task of schizoanalysis, requires an open-ended and open-minded investigation. Every user has a singular form of investment in and on the Internet. There are no foregone conclusions in the sphere of social media, which is an unsurprising oversight in the encounter between those who have grown up on social media and those who have not. Even if it is not its overt task, as when one records a private note, for example, all social media requires an industrialized act of relational self-performance. The user is invited to explore its own desiring-machines as a function of its distinction, online.

As it stands now, the mirror of big data is only indirectly held up to the user by way of who and what they see in their feed (and when). Though, connected applications track and monitor the biological and environmental conditions of the user, making autobiographical patterns that were previously impossible to recognize actionable and available directly. The move from Facebook's characteristic, web 2.0 solicitations for response and engagement to sensor-attached biometers (measuring heart rate, galvanic skin response, sleep, environmental pollutants, temperature, water quality, and others) corresponds to the move in psychology beyond talk and interview data and toward more aggressively depth-plunging, speech-evading, neurological and biological quantitative measures of human beings that trouble humanist notions of privacy, dignity, and coherent unity of the organism in the face of infinite environmental variables that trouble the boundary between self, other, and world.

Artificial individualization of users

The machinic processes of social media give way to the strange industrialization of subjective facets of life. It is now a global economic imperative that subjects deliver up, again, not enjoyment in its positive connotation of pleasure, but a dynamic "inner life" of affect that manifests as displays of agency in the world that are to be taken together as one's brand. It is the direct colonization of users as a pulsing, flowing desiring-machine, with its irruptions, twists, turns, and catatonias approximated, through translation, and accommodated as data objects on the platform. Again, the forces of subjectivation of wanting and desiring are, from the perspective of capital, not lacking, but fully utile. It is as if the productive force of interiority was tamed and disciplined only to await the cashing in on an explosion of raucous signifying energy. The speeding up of the ongoing process of desiring subjectivity must create speculative profit and increase the speed of the circulation of capital. Here desire is truly mobilized as an active, living force, over and above mere pacifying consumption. Ironically given the imperative to serve up a compelling inner life, the features of the social media interface and sorting work of its algorithms tacitly designate the parts of the user that will be commercialized and deemed suitable for others, and those that will not, which is to say, it determines the "inner" and the "outer" of selfhood and adjudicates between shareable and private affects and experiences, and between the parts of social life that are represented to others and how this occurs. We explore this further in Chapter Six.

Before platforms determine those parts of the self that are reproducible or digestible according to its norms and standards, users are first summoned as global persons and hailed by the imperative to migrate on-line, which is to say, *to be*. This takes on the form of preservation when one wants to use social media to stay connected with people who have already migrated there. This is also to say that the commodification of social relations puts on display the reliance on the Other for a self, through the subject's broaching of an absence of self and other activated in searching, posting, and responding. Brought together in, for example, Facebook's manor, the commodified self-performance process is modularized and dispersed, distributed across a sometimes very vast series of relationships or "weak ties."

On Facebook, everything begins with (and, crucially, remains tethered to) one's legal identity. On the private enclosure of the social world that is Facebook, real identity is, perversely, a requirement for entrance. Mark Zuckerberg asks that we have one true identity that must be used for our Facebook profiles. It is only by arriving as one's legally defined, unified self that the platform can be kept safe and operate as a "true community." In Kirkpatrick's (2011) book on the company's origins, Zuckerberg is quoted at a 2009 conference as saying:

> You have one identity ... The days of you having a different image for your work friends or co-workers and for the other people you know are probably coming to an end pretty quickly... Having two identities for yourself is an example of a lack of integrity. (p. 89)

The ethos of sharing, participating, and "community" ensure that we construct "real" selves to use as avatars of exchange, where such an imperative operates as a civic call for integrity. Facebook aims to reproduce credible identities that, intentionally or not, recapitulate and make legible the "performative iteration of [unmistakable] origins" (Mitropoulos, 2012, p. 65). Users are supposed to represent first according to the dictates of location, name, age, and sex. Neither does it matter very much if we are given more options to express our unique racial, sexual, or spiritual identities – to the extent that these categories have sufficient numbers, they are only used to make and amplify correlations between these and other categorical markers upstream (age, location) and downstream (searching and browsing habits) from them. Such categorization, even when not acceded to fully by the user, but inferred, is divisive; strict silos create classes of users that correspond to categories used off-line to discriminate between people (e.g., race, class, gender, sexual preference, political opinions, etc.). Unfortunately, with these raised stakes, self-production through inconsequential avatars is now a piece of Internet history. Alongside seeking, making, relating, responding, and the myriad uses to which social media are put, users are also asked to recreate their tether to states and capital. Social relating (and its vectors of self-production) is held in accounts also connected to exploitable identifiers whether awareness of this fact recedes from consciousness or is papered over by the dazzle and lures of the social web.

In this way, extremely asymmetrical social relations end up sustained by a technical system of peers. In other words, because the Internet implements a collectivity of equally powerful peers by design, the privileged access points, and modes of control on which capitalism depends are engineered atop these technical possibilities. Identification and the effort to tie users to individual human beings by IP addresses, click paths, search histories, avatars, online IDs, or even just searchable mobile cellular devices is not a technological necessity, but an accommodation of the logic of control via identity. Such control pertains to paranoiac, fascizing tendencies, whether they are understood to emanate from within or seize and restrain from without.

The mandate of one real identity tied to the contextual histories and irreversible records that come with names makes an uncountable or anonymous virtual identity implausible. With this imperative in place and Zuckerberg's conviction that the profitability of the company depends on users bringing their real identities, there is also a very real extension of social life in the process of its commodification. This real identity is hystericized as the user needs to know more to be able to act as multiple coexisting social identities in the context-meld of the platform. On-line more generally, but specifically in the catch-all social factory that is Facebook, the same spatial representation is the site of one's scholarship, one's family relationships, one's professional life, and other roles that, accordingly, combine and separate in various ways. One might therefore consider different social subjective roles; for political thinkers, Facebook is a possible state dossier, for precarious writers and media professionals it is a resume for the future of real employment, for business owners it is the locus of attraction and visibility, for public relations and communications workers it is where emotional investments are shaped and maintained, and on and on.

Individualization is not only to the detriment of the mental ecology of individuals but to users as a collectivity and social ecology. As if to prove the imaginary nature of these identifications, one can see them subordinated to the mandated "real" identity of one's account. If one is conscious of its linking to one's other online accounts (e.g., when an ad pops up on Facebook from something one searched on Google) it quickly becomes apparent that something like a true online identity is opaque to users by design. The multiple identities that all coincide on the platform, nevertheless, are abundantly present to the user even if they are not recognized as such. Despite that tantalizing sea of novelties (images, videos, texts, live streams, events, and stories), the various relationships, commitments, and professions in the life of the user limit what can be expressed on the platform. This effect of surveillance of the vertical and horizontal kinds that social media enables is known as social chilling. Because we do not know exactly by whom we are watched, only that we are made visible, the expression is forced into the lowest common denominator of a set of identities – such is the mandate to be one true identity in a context of opaque surveillance creep.

Moving forward, we see how the construction of this "real" self through both signifying and a-signifying behavior is recorded, and issues back into Facebook's primary asset, a socio-empirical data mass called the social graph. Zooming out from the subject's production of the real, identifying account, one sees that we are data- objects just like any other, for which purpose we are requisitely constructed as such unified, context-undifferentiated individuals. This is also to say that we construct and are constructed as images for others, on-line. The linkage of these images and the bodies of data tethered to them with physical IP addresses complete the tethering of the online self to the real bodies of users.

5

EXTRACTION MACHINE OF SOCIAL MEDIA

Extraction machine of social media

In the early days of the pre-corporate Internet, peer-to-peer networks exposed threads of productive relations independent of hierarchical power, state and capitalist control over reproduction, and asymmetric networks of information. Today these networks are sufficiently enclosed through relations of private property, constituting cybernetic capitalism of their de- and re-coding of the capitalist axiomatic. Schematically speaking, the massive deterritorialization of flows of information afforded by universal networking protocols and digital technologies became subject to the paranoiac, fascizing tendencies of class interest. Deleuze and Guattari's writings on faciality (e.g., 1987 Chapter 7) describe a mode of capture by which the *face* of the despot, in all its humanity, fixed and imposed meaning, stopping the slide of the signifier. Today, however, control is imposed in the readout of software interfaces, the opaque, algorithmic authority that underlies them, delimiting what the user sees and understands, and the "diagrammatic semiotics" that turns this selective visibility into actionable affordances and limitations of the physical environment.

Digital technologies function as a comparative, modulatory tool for the flow of global capital. To understand the human–machine coupling about which psychologists express concern under the banner of "Internet Addiction," we must look at the workings of the social media machine. Of what does this human–machine assemblage consist, and under what social, economic, and political conditions does it operate? What does the composition of this machinic assemblage do to its human, psychical, and social inputs? Just like doorways, fences, and international borders before them, software interfaces are thresholds that condition exchange between complex systems, playing a determinative role in the degree to which these exchanges are prohibitive or provocative, or symmetrical or asymmetrical (Bratton, 2015). The exciting thing about computational interfaces in a cybernetic regime is that they turn *representational images* into actionable technologies. The user interface is most familiar as a pointable and clickable menu of actions that a user can activate. When it comes to software interfaces, the "map" is therefore capable, to a greater or lesser extent, of reprogramming the "territory." However, the interface shows the user what they can or cannot do, or can or cannot modulate, in the perpetual becoming-actual of the virtual. Guattari (2013) would describe this semiotic type as a "diagrammatic semiotic component," where "form" operates directly on "matter".

Software guides users through a set of possible, predetermined inputs, and the platform acts as an active threshold mediating between states (Galloway, 2012). Moreover, computing is premised on the notion that objects are subject to definition and manipulation according to a set of principles for action. The matter at hand is not that of coming to know a world, but that of how specific, abstract definitions are executed to form a world. In other words, it is not exactly right to say that the platform is a formal medium, and thus declare that formalism is the appropriate way to approach it. Instead, the computer is a *formalizing* medium — like other media, it cannot address a world that is anything but entirely formalized — and because of this, it must be approached through the meeting point between world and formal model. In dealing with the capture and production of social information, we deal fundamentally with the active process of control and modulation of self and world.

These interfaces, by naming and addressing what is linked invisibly by distributed computing systems, "connect and disconnect in equal measure, structuring flows by combining and segmenting it, enabling it or frustrating it, bridging unlike forms over vast distances and subdividing that which would otherwise congeal on its own" (Bratton, 2015, p. 228). Undoubtedly, the purposely reductionistic and selective description of interfaces becomes both instrumental and totalizing because they also make projective claims that alter what they care to make visible. The digital world is full of overlapping interfaces that generate their own complexity for users; they each project different total and actionable portraits of the world. Representations are now actionable, but who represents for whom? Note that the combining and segmenting of flows and the alterations to agency that these actions enact take place *through* interfaces. While de- and re-coding of flows constitute user-interface interaction, the *frame* of these de- and re-coding, like the different platforms and protocols that *distribute* interfaces, are enclosed through preconscious class interests.

Deleuze and Guattari might have described social media platforms as *collective assemblages of enunciation*, a subset of an assemblage of desiring-production. The notion of assemblages helpfully articulates the mutual alteration of machines, the assemblages to which they connect, and the higher unity (yet another machine) composed by such linkages (Harper & Savat, 2016). A collective assemblage of enunciation is nominally defined as a redundant complex of act and statement that accomplishes it and points to the immanent relationship of language and action. They are multi-agent organs for enunciation that distribute agency across space, time, inorganic, and organic materials. Collective assemblages of enunciation like Facebook distinguish only superficially between individuals and groups - these are equalized as "accounts" on social media. In the notion of Internet Addiction, just as much as in other techno-fetishistic ideas about social media, the platform as a *process* is mistaken for a *thing* and mislabeled as a reified object (in this case, a "free" commodity) that encounters a passive and addicted subject.

Social media, then, is not merely a reflection of the world, but what has become of the experience of the world, which itself creates worlds. The extension of social media itself into increased parts of the world is a testament to its capacity for insertion in other assemblages. Nevertheless, it constitutes a distinctive exportation of American culture. The rise of social media platforms has undoubtedly had profound influences (both in its concept and style and its international lobbying efforts) on other sites of production of language, affects, and codes. It draws together many different forms of networked production in terms of the social constraints and affordances it generates. Looking at the dynamics of Facebook allows us to outline more clearly interventions that do not pit the subject against the agency of the network, but enable a livable relationship to it, within it. Facebook is one major player in what Bratton (2015) calls the "Cloud polis." By this, he means:

> The model provided and enacted by global cloud platforms to cohere Users into proto-state entities. These entities may operate at the scale of a true state and may come into political geographic conflict with states accordingly. *Cloud polis* is characterized by hybrid geographies, incomplete governmental apparatuses, awkward jurisdictions, new regimes of interfaciality, archaic imagined communities, group allegiances, ad hoc patriotisms, and inviolable brand loyalties … We can observe different formal models of *Cloud polis* in the service architectures of contemporary

> *Cloud* platforms, such as Google, Amazon, Facebook, and Apple, and can deduce possible *Cloud polis* by the recombination of these architectures. (pp. 369–370)

Facebook is one of the current cloud platform empires, though the way it exists today is by no means determinative of future arrangements of its stakeholders. As one of a handful of significant ventures, it can be viewed as a prototype for geopolitical cloud futures. What sets Facebook apart and makes it especially interesting is that, in addition to being an oft-named subset of Internet Addiction (social media addiction, Facebook addiction), it is also a cloud polis built from the lives of its users. This moves to the fore questions of human interest related to ubiquitous network technology at layers beyond those visible to users (e.g., the energy expenditure of data centers or technical re-orientation of supply chains).

Facebook is not only a player of the cloud polis. It is also a platform, as its representatives have claimed numerous times in the face of allegations that they should take on responsibilities like ensuring the spread of good journalism, reducing misinformation, and maintaining specific standards of content. Taking representatives of Facebook and CEO Mark Zuckerberg at his word, then, requires us to ask what, exactly, is a platform? Platforms are not merely technical models, but institutional forms on par with states and markets. They are generative of interaction. They set terms of participation according to fixed protocols, whose value paradoxically lies in their ability to mediate interactions that may not be conceivable from the outset of their design. Platforms remotely coordinate and control the distribution of interfaces. Platforms have the capacity, therefore, to transform social processes according to their own logic, in advance of, and as a result of, their use — provided that such social processes are dependent upon them in the first place. Applications that are accessed by users are, in fact, byte-sized platforms that link individual devices to large databases contained in the massive storage and processing centers that we familiarly call the "cloud."

Because platforms act as major "hubs," or attractors of most traffic online, the logic of executable knowledge extends to all of the social platforms that make up "Web 2.0." This is to say that what we call the Internet in its non-technological specification is essentially just social media. Social media is, in turn, a privileged site of producing and reproducing social relations under the auspices of a business' profit-driven logic. The companies that operate social media, like most other forms of media, comprise the primary network participation of most users today. Facebook is a blockbuster or "oligopolistic" software. As such, it is a cultural text that frames forms of user interaction, determining the terms of our social relations with a billion other users, all the way down to how electrical signals are routed to our devices. In a world of competitive social platforms, users find themselves governed by algorithmic decision-making machines that differentiate the platforms and are themselves forged of unique couplings, fissures, and accidents of states and markets to which they cannot be reduced. These platforms are the ultimate arbiters of how interfaces "treat" different users; they decide what the user can do and when, and significantly condition the routes by which actions by the user proceed. The next section looks at how Facebook arrived at this degree of social power.

Facebook and the profit motive

Facebook is among the winners of "Web 2.0" businesses. Web 2.0 is distinguished from the earlier Internet atmosphere by its ease of use, direct facilitation of sociality, and free publishing and production platforms that allow users to upload content in any form of their choosing (Lovink, 2011). Web 2.0 and its features follow from the dot.com crash. At this time, Google made waves by developing a means to profit solely based on free, user-generated content, or as they say, by attempting to "organize the world's information." Web 2.0, in its rhetoric as much as its technical infrastructure, embeds principles of participation and interactivity assured by inter-operability between different platform — another feature that heightens users' capacity to distribute information.

Tim Berners-Lee, credited with the invention of the World Wide Web, lucidly articulated that the dream behind the early Internet was to communicate, through sharing information, in a common space (Kennedy, 2013). Facebook also claims to want us to be able to share information more efficiently. It is this rhetoric that partially establishes social media giants' function as hosts of the party, so to speak or the new facilitators of the social world. By emphasizing their role as social facilitators, the politics of data labor, management, ownership, and monetization are conveniently stored away, and political-economic issues are overwritten as largely technocratic ones (Gillespie, 2010). The company line, abetted by a twisted version of the 90s net-cultural ethos of sharing, serves first to obscure proprietary control, and then to neutralize and smooth out the relations between the content-generating users, the platform vectoralists, and the advertisers and data handlers who put it to intermediary uses (Kennedy, 2013). Facebook navigates the open sharing ethos of the early Internet and web 2.0, and the content industry, which seeks to "close" computer code and media content by asserting intellectual property rights. Such navigation is a great demonstration of the antagonism between information as a common good and information as the key commodity in digital capitalism.

Web 2.0 is less a set of innovative technologies than it is a new model of behavior. Its features created a cut in the elite information sharing of universities and government intelligence agencies to facilitate behaviors often associated with a more mundane sociality; attracting the attention of others in one's milieu, recounting and circulating signs of eating, sleeping, exercising, purchasing, etc. Chatting, posting, texting, sharing pictures, videos, and whatever else with our network contacts (and beyond) was all part of the zeitgeist of a new and exciting online world in the early to mid-2000s (Ippolita Collective et al., 2009). In its guise as a participatory world, its more recent progression mostly fails to distinguish the participatory contributions of people and devices. The so-called "Internet of Things" relies increasingly on data collection from "agents" for services provided off-line (Weber & Wong, 2017). We could imagine, for example, a chair that can sense how much you like sitting on it, your seated heart rate, galvanic skin response, and the amount of time you have spent sitting, filtering into Facebook ads for the fitness franchise nearest to your home.

It is not as if popular media outlets do not expose the exploitative or predatory nature of social media, in its links with advertising agencies, data brokers, and analysts. Recall the Cambridge Analytica voter manipulation scandal of 2014–2018, and the leaked emails evincing surveillance efforts of U.S. police departments and the National Security Agency. However, these phenomena tend to be presented as hiccups in an otherwise egalitarian trade-off between user and web company. The overarching story of the participatory web, Web 2.0, costs a little privacy to have the convenience of an instant communication and social discovery service. This story centers the conversation on whether Facebook is a good consumer choice, suggesting that a cost-benefit analysis of the platform is tipped in the direction of benefits. To take an example of how this decision-making process proceeds: A 2017 report states that a comparison between the free political Facebook news content and traditional news outlets demonstrated that Facebook news is superior in terms of entertainment and killing time, but for parameters like "balanced information" and "social utility," Facebook pales in comparison (Schäfer et al., 2017).

Facebook and other web and tech companies are deeply embroiled in the rise of financialization that has been the hallmark of neoliberal societies since the 1970s. Understanding the user from a critical, whole systems perspective requires this kind of connection-making and an understanding of the degree to which inflating stock valuations crucially informs the mode of expression available to the user and intensification of user intrigue and interest. Greg Elmer (2017) suggests a critical approach to Internet history in which one looks at the process of web companies' financialization. In times leading up to significant rounds of funding that Elmer calls "pre-corporation," architects were designing to pursue future interests, coming out with new directions and features of the platform. As we have said, Facebook is such a major force on-line that this view allows one to extrapolate about the direction of network production writ large, shaped as it is by the projections, features, and profit-creation of its leading companies. In the case of Facebook, such value is, of course, sought in social networking.

Pre-corporation is the moment when investors must be convinced to part with their money. This is the development of the specifics of network production because its inventors must discern a processual way of selling and profiting from the coordination of social relations. When the question of value is "immaterial," instead of a more tangible, landed asset, it can be a mostly obscure matter that eludes critics and market-watchers alike. Taking advantage of the ethereal, non-visible facet of production abstracted from concrete goods, and the vaporous, highly mobile quality of data, it is difficult to grasp its course even for those with vested interest in doing so.

As the dotcom gold rush cascaded forwarded, leading to the dot-bomb market crash of 1999 and 2000, pre-corporate histories of the Internet also became governmental stories, highlighting the rules that dictate the conditions of pre-corporate promotions, offers, "pitches," and trades. Brian Murphy (2002) reminds us that since the late 1990s, the Internet has been governed as a for-profit commercial sphere. While earlier forms of what is now the Internet (Arpanet) were developed for academic and military use by the Defense Advanced Research Projects Agency (DARPA) of the U.S. Department of Defense decades earlier, Vice President Al Gore shepherded a series of government bills that would place control of the Internet in the hands of the private sector. The primary enabling legislation, the Communications Act of 1996, governed the operations of all media in the United States, affirming that "the Market will drive both the internet and information highway" (*ibid*, p. 31). What this has amounted to over the last couple of decades is that massive public investment of taxpayer money has funded the infrastructure on top of which companies extract value very inexpensively (Frischmann, 2013; Mazzucato, 2018).

Facebook's prospectus, the key document used to sell the company's future financial viability and worth to investors and the market, was revised six times to arrive at a basic model of market viability (Blodget, 2012). In each instance, revisions were sought by market regulators and financial underwriters like Morgan Stanley, J. P. Morgan, and Goldman Sachs, to sharpen the case for how the company would go about making money. While most recognized that ad sales would lead the way for Facebook, revisions to the prospectus also noted the role of the company's recently developed "social graph" algorithm — in conjunction with the roll-out of a mobile platform — would enhance the company's prospects. To prevent aggravation from future social networks, its makers created a developer platform, allowing programmers to build apps capable of running on top of, rather than in competition with, Facebook. The combination of the network's mobility (people can use it all the time, everywhere), its warding off of competition by making it easier for aspiring network capitalists to establish their footing as sub-networks of Facebook, and the patenting of the means to allow the network to self-capitalize (the social graph that refines data as to make it valuable) was the perfect recipe.

While the process of seeking investment is most clearly associated with the process of financialization (seeking investment through the stock market), almost all Internet companies share a pre-corporate period of external capitalization and investment, often by these so-called "angel investors," or by other larger digital media and software companies like Google and Microsoft, who take a small stake or ownership in the emerging firm. The years of pre-corporation are closely attuned to market regulations of the day, the rules that define the responsibilities and processes that incorporated, public companies must follow. The writing and rewriting of the company's prospectus were chiefly governed by the U.S. Securities Act and overseen by the Securities and Exchange Commission. In addition to questions of immaterial value, IPO sales, and market regulation, Facebook also used its pre-corporate years, specifically 2008–2012, leading up to the NASDAQ IPO, to reconfigure its relationship with its technicians and programmers. Compared to other on-line moguls, Facebook always had a startlingly small number of employees, and during their pre-corporate phase, the company only formally employed about 3,000 people. However, this figure is misleading when one considers the 835 million users on whom it depends on ad revenue and the production of social data (Thompson, 2012).

Facebook changed its attitude toward its content-providing user base to intensify its efforts to collect the data needed to make the social graph valuable — the more data, the more powerful the social graph algorithm, and the more valuable Facebook becomes. The pre-corporate era, then, became synonymous with rapid changes in the interface's aesthetics for addressing users, its functions, and its features. In the case of Facebook, all these changes amount to ways of intensifying user surveillance and data mining, particularly immediately preceding their stock flotation. Right around the time of pre-corporation, in 2011, it was even revealed that

Facebook makes "ghost" or "shadow" profiles for people they hope will eventually become users, and link these profiles with identifying information gathered from other parts of the Internet.

By 2010, twelve months before the company IPO, the platform witnessed 48 changes, many focused on promoting more networking with other users, tagging friends in updates, uploading photos, alerting users to "friend anniversaries," and so forth. Most importantly for the future prospectus of Facebook was the introduction of the open graph protocol in April of 2010, where all objects, users, non-users, media, and text were integrated into Facebook's back-end algorithms and data mining technologies. In many cases, the changes were experienced by users as prompts that encouraged them to post more, upload more, and engage with their friend networks through ever more granular means. That's a lot of social labor! From the perspective of competition among social platforms to procure relative surplus-value, the heightened productivity of labor is akin to keeping users on the platform and getting them to create themselves via representation and communication, on the one hand, but also social acts that are not traditionally asserted or registered, like viewing, hovering, and lurking.

Changes that prompt ever greater opportunities for self-performance and monitoring often occur without protest, as an overwhelming majority of users accept default settings of social network platforms and almost all users adopt new settings without complaint (Shepherd & Landry, 2013). In fact, critics like Frischmann and Selinger (2018) have suggested that the defining change wrought by ubiquitous network platforms is the multiplication of contractual agreements in the form of boilerplate contracts. These boilerplate contracts are designed to be sped through, such that reading the text in them is difficult, inconvenient, and can be easily avoided by clicking "I agree" and moving on to the experience offered by the platform or service.

When Facebook's privacy policy proudly proclaims that it has never and will never sell our information, it is because it would be fiscally nonsensical to dispossess themselves of the market-guiding and predictive power associated with granting or withholding access to that data (Kennedy, 2013). The business of gathering data centers on a sound plan to own it rather than to sell it, meaning that we should expect, just as we have seen in the precorporate era, concerted efforts to cultivate such data in both breadth and scale. This process is also structurally transformative of commercial media because, instead of being funded by advertising, it will be funded through commercialized, personal data (Patelis, 2013). Rather than just being paid by advertisers in exchange for viewers' attention, social media can sell data directly to interested companies for other social purposes and more serious ones, like establishing credit ratings and insurance premiums.

Unlike traditional media companies that create and distribute information in the form of paid content, Facebook organizes, filters, and distributes unpaid content that they solicit by spurring our virtual, imaginative capacities for envisioning society at large. The network company refused to revise their sorely inadequate form of data encryption upon a case filed against it by the Belgian data protection commission in the wake of the Court of Justice of the European Union's 2014 ruling on the misleadingly titled "Right to Be Forgotten" case. This speaks to Facebook's implicit necessity to deny or deflect concerns about surveillance and tracking, among other nefarious uses of the data it harvests. Companies like Facebook that control on-line information that flows on such a grand scale are new kinds of business entities and need to be treated as such by the public and its institutions. The opacity of its data-processing protocols that the proposed deletion of data by users outed is a strong testament to the stark power asymmetry between the company and the "prosumers" whose work of connection it carefully crafts.

Vectoralist power

It is worth repeating the way that Wark (2004) has parsed this out, developing a notion of the rentier model of telecommunication quite fully, which culminates in an exposition of the "vectoralist class." Like its usage in epidemiology, a vector is the channel through which something travels. They also denote any means by which information moves. Simultaneously, as telecommunications name the capacity for perception at a distance, they also name particular vectors, like the telegraph or telephone. While any particular media vector has fixed properties, like bandwidth, scope, and speed, its uneven development may be viewed as a function of political economy rather than technical possibility. Vectoralist commodification may occur at the level of information stocks, flows, or even vectors themselves for telecommunications companies (i.e., AT&T). The commodification of information such that surplus-value may be extracted from it requires transporting information through space and time.

Accordingly, this archival mass, big data, is a vector through time as "communication is a vector that crosses space" (Wark, 2004, abst. 24). Such an archive has enduring value and is maintained through time – hence its commensurately greater effect on the lives of users. On Facebook, a flow of information denotes the capacity to extract and distribute information of temporary value out of action on, mediated by, or otherwise monitored through the platform. Vectoralists own platforms in the sense that they control and govern the platform, walling off the algorithms that make it, along with the information users provide intentionally or unintentionally. Vectoral power rides atop pastoral power in its ownership, not of the information specifically, but of value based on its distribution in time. It is in this sense that class-based oppression might be understood as only one particular fetish in the larger struggle to organize the totality of human effort (Wark, 2015). Note that the power of the vectoralists is not explicitly cognitive, but thrives equally on volatility and bad information as on intelligence and reason, and makes no distinction between tracking these faculties of the user and its sexual and corporeal inclinations. Conscious intentions? Unconscious movement? To the vectoralist, it is all just data in their coffers.

Everything we type, "like," and click is on the land of the vectoralists, and in the house of platform owners. The user signals to other users through direct and indirect address, but also beyond the inter-subjective instances of communication that occur on the visible interface. They also signal perpetually and unknowingly to a "vertical" other, a sort of semi-personified God (the platform, the algorithm) that registers everything, all the time. The semiotics of information and data production, users, and the capitalist production of surplus-value of selves operate in concert. In the digital economy of which social media and the whole of the Internet are a part, the surplus value (money made) by users just *being there* is unevenly distributed between those from whom it is extracted, users, and those who extract it, the vectoralists.

The dynamics of monopolistic ownership, value extraction, labor exploitation and precariousness, power-law distribution (simply called network effects) are, for some, reminiscent of the robber baron-age monopolies of the early 1900s (e.g., Burbach et al., 2001; Hodges, 2000; Morozov, 2015). Similarly, if one takes the spatial metaphor of the Internet seriously, it is equally apparent that the capture of social substance (linguistic, affective, symbolic, and cultural commons) in platform enclosures shares qualities with the pre-capitalist feudal manors where peasants worked an enclosed space at the hands of lords in exchange for sustenance.

With the distance between the people represented by accounts, a standardization of form moves in. The software creates a form to be filled in that structures the process of self-ing. This standardization into code of self-building practices and top-down curation of sociality is a power grab by vectoralists who appropriate social life as raw material: one can look at this raw material as the user becoming an asset, both laboring but also simply *being* as an (objectified) asset in a profit-driven game. The movie *The Social*

Network (Brunetti et al., 2010) offers us a superficial glimpse into its founding from the perspective of the manufacture of the platform and its use-value. The first scene of the film portrays a male student, who we quickly learn attends Harvard, asking his love interest how one is supposed to distinguish oneself from a population of people who all got the 1600s (the then-highest score) on their SATs. She is then portrayed breaking up with him moments after, "not because [he's] a nerd, but because [he's] an ass-hole." Struggling with the desire to stand out, he creates Facebook for the express purpose of keeping tabs on his now-ex-girlfriend (while also being able to rate and rank the hotness of other college girls). Stalking and lurking, both descriptors for common usage of social media, especially Facebook, at which no one even bats an eye, are the foundational rather than deviant or transgressive uses of the platform, and the term "surveillance" denotes the same type of use at even greater degrees of organization.

Controversies surrounding Facebook's own practices of sharing data show that manipulating consumer behavior is secondary to the imperatives of capitalism more broadly. The company's obligation to its shareholders to grow and profit wholly dictates with whom its data assets are shared: it strategically gives access to other tech giants like Microsoft, Amazon, Yahoo, and Apple and sells user attention to advertisers and other interests in information's select distribution. What is important in the grand scheme of things is that the creation of the silos that lock data-producing users in an anxious environment of awkward timing, faceless social interactions, and incalculable consequences is secondary to the appropriation of surplus-value — a sort of insider information of everything, everywhere — on offer to states as much as to advertisers. The question of ownership and access by necessity operates and therefore must be thought about before attempts to control what is said or who says what, on-line.

When we send information through the vectoralists' channels, we "speak their language" at *every level except that of meaning*. A user may send a message on Facebook to a friend to ask them if they can meet at such and such a time. This message may be received and responded to in the affirmative. What's the problem here? It is that that message is duplicated: one's friend gets a copy, and Facebook keeps one, too. This means that to participate in the sort of horizontal, libidinal economy that is visible on Facebook, one must also devote this participation to the unknowable purposes for which Facebook itself maps and trust their decisions about who else will get to see this information — their data ethics. Even when we experience our recycled activity in the form of suggestion (i.e., the superego incarnate), such suggestion is over-determined by these interests. The almighty algorithm, then, poses as a neutral adjudicator of the fate-and-chance ethos of the social world, even as relative degrees of visibility is largely determined by the joint requirements of unhinging and sustaining the desire of users and selling exposure directly.

Given the capitalist axiomatic of de- and re-territorialization, digitization may be thought of as an ongoing process by which signifiers either become commodities (e.g., names are digital spaces, and function to some degree as land, at the same time as software code is considered both a good and a service), or they are inextricably linked to the capitalist axiomatic. On the one hand, the perfusion of signifiers becomes a sign of the entire enterprise of social media, signaling its future value. Because Facebook primarily sells ad space, the assumption is that more use, that is, more attention it can capture, equates to its greater value as an advertising vehicle. This value is expressed numerically as revenue and stock price. On the other hand, signifiers become market information, valuable in production for production's sake on their own as a signal of what the user wants or what the user could be made to want (with the aid of some gentle nudging, of course). This becoming market information of the signifier also heralds an algorithmic organization that groups users and the information they generate and to which they are linked.

Because these monopolists of communication infrastructure operate both before and after the production of physical goods and rendering of services, social media's value lies in providing infrastructure through which identifications are made. These identifications foster aspirations to new lifestyles and expressions. As users compete for attention on social media platforms, advertising gains ontological ground. Because it is constructed to keep users using, which is to say, being themselves, the idea is to make it as captivating as possible, sort of like hypnosis that begins first with induction and then with an entrance into difficult or sensitive subjects. This works well because the unconscious of living, active force belongs to the collective assemblage of enunciation rather than the individual — even as the individual account operates as a perpetual point of return, the "territorial unconscious" of the assemblage.

6
DATA COLLECTION AND THE RELATIONAL FACTORY

Dependence and lock-in

In Facebook's efforts to incorporate, the need to attract more users to the platform, as to build it up with user data, drove its major design features. Most of these took the form of programmed pleas that users self-position and represent in ever greater degrees of detail, as when one can choose from hundreds of different moods to select and display, and by making suggestions for action, as when the platform suggests that you tag your friends' faces in newly uploaded photos. All that mattered for Facebook at the time of pre-corporation was increasing the number of connections between people (as data objects, or corollaries of digital devices). The connections users make between one another are over-determined by Facebook's inter-mediation. This is because Facebook and other social media are what technologist Stephen Wolfram, in a testimony to the U.S. Senate, called "automated content selection businesses." They attract and incite large swaths of semiotic data (content) to use artificial intelligence to automatically determine what to deliver, to whom, and when. Such determinations are based on the data they have previously been able to capture from users.

Facebook creates a social computing environment from users' "raw material." By keeping this foothold of user investment, as if distracting users with commodified versions of each other, they are then subordinated to the motivations and whims of the platform's self-subsistence. In some circumstances, this amassing of connected users under its dominion is more obvious than others. In its (failed) "Free Basics" program, Facebook aimed to become a one-stop Internet shop — the exclusive portal to the whole of the web — in rural India and some countries in the Global South. As an apparatus of capture, Facebook is in the business of appropriating sociality for miniature activities of uploading, tagging, registering, and evaluating that increase its power as a corporate entity.

Does this global social infrastructure that is mainstream social media have to do with the ambition of the corporations in charge of them, with the tendency toward structural inequality on the web, or both? The tendency toward activity concentrated in major hubs is called the "predictable imbalance" of the Pareto Principle (see Sanders, 1987). For a more thorough understanding, we must also look at what are called "network effects," described by libertarian tech mogul and Facebook board member, Peter Thiel, in his instructions to Stanford University undergraduates on "how to create a network monopoly." Large, scalable networks create network topologies with an asymmetric, highly unequal distribution that, at the level of IP (the router network), follows a power law quite closely (Barabási & Bonabeau, 2003). Such a network structure consists of a collection of non-uniformly connected nodes. The connectors of these islands of nodes are called hubs, and the role of the hub goes to enormous databases and our top social media sites. A small number of strongly connected and many weakly connected objects enables an exceedingly small network diameter with very many nodes without an overall extremely high degree of connectivity. Massively connected nodes enable great leaps and provide for the overall cohesion of the network. As a major node, Facebook reaches about 73% of all Internet users, trumped only by Google.

Unevenness is the most important ingredient of ultra-scalable networks — they are driven with the help of databases. When nodes are added to scale-free networks, they preferentially attach themselves to highly connected nodes, prompting the celebrity culture of Facebook and other social media at the level of its data-collecting infrastructure. This descriptive law of networks gives rise to the phenomenon of platform monopolies at the corporate level as it does to influencers (persona nodes so highly connected that they are paid by companies to promote them) on the individual level. Facebook's proprietary "social graph" ensures that all data produced through Facebook's incursion into the Internet at large stays in its clutches produced as a sign of its future value to shareholders. Facebook, like Google, Amazon, Alibaba, Twitter, and Instagram, are not simply ideas that can be aped, as per traditional forms of market competition that aim to better serve users. Rather, we must keep in mind that these monopolies are entrenched global infrastructures that draw together financial actors, private investors, and state governing bodies, in addition to users.

Society-wide dependence and social media's shaping of social interactions makes exit and entrance dynamics key sites of struggle for users and groups (Bratton, 2015). As Morozov (2015) says, we cannot leave Facebook for an improved but roughly commensurate social media site because of its network dominance and the corporate-monopolistic stronghold over the index it has created. The difficulties of the little known, federated social media alternatives, like Mastodon or Diaspora, in garnering support for its non-monetized and open-source project is telling of just how harrowing it is to compete for users against a company that is and has been reaping the benefits of network effects of primacy (Sevignani, 2013). Nothing less than a collective, simultaneous movement away from the platform, a break in the habit, could effectively break the primacy of the network effects from which Facebook creates "lock-in." This lock-in functions through the dialectical relationship between communication and social space. It has been noted in the social cognitive and affective neuroscience literature that our social reputations are as precious to us as our bodies, and that we feel pain in a similar way to both kinds of injury (Novembre et al., 2015). It is therefore the hoarding of user-produced assets *including relationships* that creates this lock-in, to the effect that your existing social relationships, friends, family, or whomever, are essentially kidnapped. This makes the platform owners and those with whom they share access rights predators of sociality *per se,* upon the psychic operations that produce social space *as* virtualities (prepared, here, for veritable colonization).

Its proprietary "social graph" explored below aims to map all social life. Apparatuses of capture contribute, from the outset to the constitution of the aggregate upon which the capture is effectuated (Deleuze & Guattari, 1987). This is precisely the objective of Facebook's social graph. Capture appears between the distributed set and the set of real goods. In this correspondence or comparison, "the power of acquisition is created in direct conjunction with the set of real productions." There is neither theft nor victim because the producer only loses what he does not have and has no chance of acquiring. The social graph is a unique digital asset upon which billions of dollars of speculation is based precisely because it promises ongoing, emergent opportunities to sell, pander to, and appropriate desires and direct the speech of the billions of users who it tracks. The world according to the social graph is a mathematical formalization of what Facebook believes users wants on the basis of past on-line behaviors, and its generic architecture for stimulating desiring-machines (e.g., the features that drive more and more productive use, like frequent alerts and a never-ending feed of curated posts). As we will see, the series of acts by which this mapping and being mapped occurs secures users as distinctive, yet pliable objects of a psychical science of relations, distances, proximities, viewing, and signifying.

Time- and effort-dependent gradations of data and information are useful ways to understand the progressive cycling of the dividual users and the commodification of its acts of online self-production. Data includes the machine-readable mélange of code, language, and behaviors like selecting, responding, various connections between users and machines, mouse-hovering, clicks, scrolls, timers, and even the time differentials between behaviors. Data is the smallest imaginable unit of value, from the perspective of the capitalist axiomatic of intellectual property creation and enclosure, and so too does it denote a raw form of expenditure that enters into the attention economy by factoring in as a storage cost on the company's servers. Information is the result of the selective processing of this data into coherent, human-readable language. It is the layer of sorting and deducing, through statistical parameterizing and application, an imaginary social totality from the perpetual movement of users milling about on and off social media platforms. Such quantizing and sense-making is the machinic process that succeeds in the collection of data through cookies, trackers, and GPS in real-time.

Deducing the value of such information is the job for Facebook's investors and clients, and the more complete the map is understood to be, the more valuable it is. Its robustness correlates to the market of all users, marking out, for powerful stakeholders, third parties, and initiatives that patronize the site, and governments to whom backdoors are frequently offered, a social world *as* that which can be engineered. This map is supposed to answer the famous question of social subjection, "what does the Other want from me?" – it gives information that would finally answer this question such that industrial production and its distribution mechanisms can know what to produce, when, and for whom, and select governing and corporate bodies are armed with the predictive power to know who is congregating, where, and when. Does this imply that these same privileged actors have access to the purposes to which user activity and behavior correspond? Do they care? The process of interpretation by which information crosses a threshold of refinement into the realm of knowledge may be outside of the scope of interest of those who have access to the greatest volume of data.

By looking more deeply at Facebook's Social Graph, we begin to see more precisely the workings of the appropriations of the self-mutative and existentially affirmative. Such appropriation carries with it the imaginary registers already implicit in objects, places, and people – their identifications, ideals, and aspirations, and adds to this mix the logic of social-empirical formalism. The protocol underlying the Social Graph allows the platform to replicate within its database a kind of semantic map of the web, based on the activity of users which first adds their friends, cataloging who is connected to whom, and then begins adding "things" they like or share. The protocol also adds "social buttons," or trackers that report back to Facebook, across the Internet. Hence the general equivocation (and purposeful demonstration) in this piece; as it stands most Internet Addictions (where there is compulsive shopping, gambling, browsing, or gaming) is also a Social Media Addiction, and more specifically, a Facebook addiction. This is because its expressly designed logic of sharing infiltrates so many (though not all) popular sites and applications. Every time a page has a "like" button it becomes captured as a Facebook object, replicated for its back-end use. The Social Graph is Facebook's source of value and serves as a sign to their shareholders of this robust social empirical knowledge. It embodies the neoliberal ideology that states that society exists only as a collection of individuals, and the knowledge produced therein is precisely the ongoing mapping of more and more of the social totality *as* a collection of unique, self-marketing, self-positioning, and self-representing individual users.

Social mapping as value production: Part one

On Facebook, the sociality that makes these accounts is transmitted unilaterally into the data citadel of the social graph. This direct transmission does not only amount to the elision of the subject via anxiety or its hyperinflation through excessive identifications. It is also an absolute version of the individual — its total coincidence with its own social subjection through the coordinates of categories meaningful for the purpose of advertising and categorizing gender, sexuality, race, class, religion. For all its impressive mathematical opacity, the algorithmic social empiricism of Facebook relies on categories laden with meaning, which are by no means neutral. Facebook's users are therefore subject to a regime of private labels that sort them into categories relevant for the vast amount of social and economic activity that exists on-line. While we retain meaning from content, the associations created through the categories, or really the encoded values of the platform are a language that comes from above. It is in this sense that users who signify are "spoken" rather than speaking nonetheless, or mute in the face of a socially powerful ledger capable of serving the aims of anyone able to access it. Note, now, that the signifying signs of the account, those that are supposed to represent the subject who produce them on-line, become object-actants (agents) by these decontextualized fragments of subjective truth, collected as bodies of global human social logs. These signs of participation are captured in the language of code, inserted into databases, processed, analyzed against each other, etc.

Deleuze once wrote that *relation* is not a property of objects and is always external to its terms. They have a spiritual or mental existence and belong to the whole rather than to objects (1986, p. 10). Relations between users imply the capacity for mutuality, or the capacity to affect and be affected by others. Yet, while the linkages between signifiers representing subjects are capitalized, the social relations of the extraction of surplus-value are obscured. While the content of our speech is an address directed toward, and indeed often read by peers, family, colleagues, and so on, the coded data that, below the level of the text, facilitates its meta-organization, storage, ownership, and future uses is directed to the corporate-owned platforms themselves. This control layer above and below subjects, turns out not only to circumvent the question of the subject but intensifies the production of mutually embedded, entropic selves produced as commodified information (Wark, 2006). Irrespective of what the capacity to affect and be affected by others means for users who comprise these relations, they are valued in the capitalist economy as the digital assets of particular social media companies. Such assets signal to investors and clients their own growing capacity to control and manipulate the behavior of users.

This value is human capital, considered from the perspective of labor, and is paid in social capital, or the *access to others, made necessary by broken ties,* considered from the perspective of users. This betweenness, not to mention the consistency of generation of valuable data outside of working spaces or traditional hours, constitutes a profound break between the capitalist temporality of "moments," considered from the perspective of value as "socially necessary labor-time." Such valuation begs the question of a temporality specific to *care* insofar as struggles over time (and, by extension, writing, and remembering) are characteristic of the capitalist mode of production (Harvey & Marx, 2010, p. 199). How much time, or what *quality of time*, does it take to maintain social connections that support the circulation of capital? And, how much of this maintenance work can be offloaded to the software itself, relative to the human user?

Perhaps a human society version of the technological singularity would be the moment at which no one can tell the difference between a human with whom they have loose enough connections to add as a Facebook friend and a fully automated version of that person. For those who are concerned about human obsolescence in the face of intelligent machines, or on the flip side, consider themselves socially anxious or mired in tedium of human relations, it is worth considering the value of software that can achieve this.

Is an empirical, demographic science of people based on their habits of consumption — of physical-object commodities as much as the images and texts produced by others — up to the task? Rather than broach these questions directly, we turn instead to what is produced, in the present, by its all-encompassing measurements of behavior. There emerges platform *lock-in* that combines (1) *dependence* on the basis of its impressive amount of users, and (2) *lost control* on the basis of the accumulation of a mass of personal data that it owns on each person and their connections with each other.

Many would consider this extraction and accumulation a genuine problem unto itself, based on a loss of privacy or dignity. The fact of the matter is that this extraction and accumulation is the basis of capital's overcoming of human labor, jumping from money to capital, or from investment to surplus without much need for enlightenment-style humans at all. This is the tendency for the organic composition of capital to increasingly favor fixed capital (machines) over variable capital (humans). The dynamic creation and movement of humans and groups, when accumulated into the social graph, may now be highly valuable for policing, public safety measures, and for the purchase of the attentive eyeballs of would-be consumers. It is also valuable, however, as an assessment of minimal human needs, to produce a minimally-surviving being who can eventually be completely done away with. Much like neuroscience provides a scientific model of the human brain to be emulated by cybernetic machines and robots, Facebook may provide modeling of groups to inform the competition between automated, capital-producing corporate entities of the future, from which the vast majority of humanity is excluded or disregarded.

The Graphical User Interface (GUI) delivers this social empirical formalism to users, presenting a clean, satisfyingly organized environment for its meanderings, its strolls, fascinations, and fixations. Nevertheless, the dogmatism of the platform's encoded laws and procedures for the collection of data is securely shielded by smooth and convenient dashboards and graphics. In a certain sense, interfaces appear to be analogous to both the traditional "veil" of ideology, obscuring the algebraic social of the machine, and acting as an opiate of the masses, providing a palliative measure to the anxiety baked into digital temporality. For example, Wendy Chun's (2011) study of real-time computer interfaces concludes that when we compute we are offered, both conceptually and thematically, a way to map and engage an increasingly complex world driven by the high speed, ever-changing rule of the informatic capitalist market. She argues that interfaces induce the user to map constantly so that the user in turn can be mapped. Everything is created as a digital object that we can control on the graphical user interface, and it is this extension of control through mapping, in addition to the delights of simulated social interaction, that constitute the veil that is the interface. Personalization and control both are meant to be amplified by ongoing improvements to interfaces, which produce the "feed," or the incessant stream of statements, images, and opinions that make up online social life.

Real and possible objects alike are modeled inside the graph. Users are encouraged to build maps of their social relations, but also to use social media software to preempt, encourage, and manifest new ones. Users are made to wrest things from their social, historical, and political contexts, and map them according to the platform's logic in a language its algorithms can learn from – we teach the platform, providing the substance of its programmatic reproduction. With the introductions of social plug-ins and buttons, a larger data structure is modeled, in which other objects (shops, cities, bands, celebrities) can become part of the graph and subject to its data processing. Zwick and Dholakia's (2006) notion of epistemic consumption objects characterizes these objects well. Epistemic consumption objects reveal themselves progressively through interaction, observation, use, examination, and evaluation. Such layered revelation is accompanied by an extension rather than a diminution of the object's complexity. In this way, its lack of ontological stability turns the object into a continuous project of self- and service- discovery for users. The ongoing cycle of revelation and discovery is at least one facet of the strong, complex attachments to platforms like Facebook. There is thus a "quasi-social" (Zwick & Dholakia, 2006) relationship to the software itself.

Marx (1939-41/1993) understood commodities as objects that mystify in that they are themselves *more than themselves*. This is because they incarnate the labor that went into their production. Value is not hidden in commodities but exists in the relationship between them as a function of the social relationships of production. Epistemic consumption objects, one must note, are equally epistemic production objects that trouble Marx's categories at the same time as they expose the veracity of his theory of value. They do not only incarnate but are actively "recharged" with social reproductive labor as a living, even mundane practice of the user. These "consumer" objects contain the means of harnessing labor power, or conscripting labor power, by means of such connectivity. An epistemic consumption object helps us consider the apex of Marx's theory of commodity fetishism, which for Kordela (2018) undermines the Kantian paradigm of the duality of things and their representations. Digital *prosumption* objects cast light on this binary-breaking reading of Marx's theory of commodity fetishism in that the simultaneous and reciprocal mutual constitution of subject and object is melded with striking conspicuousness. Even the design of early computing components that we take for granted, like the mouse and the keyboard, lump together generating and retrieving information as actions afforded to (and expected of) users.

For Fuchs (2019), commodity fetishism is inverted on social media platforms because social relations veil the commodity form of software rather than commodities veiling the social relations that go into their production. This is exactly what is happening when social media and the Internet is considered a product or as an object of consumption. What is missed is not just labor incarnated in an object, but also the housing of social life itself. Excessive use of social media exists only within a social economy of flows that pass through and between users. The process of enslavement becomes the premise of capitalism more clearly, in the sense of enslavement to something larger than oneself. Multiple interwoven selves that fly under the banner of the individual are what is being commodified – not as labor, but as the finished product of a series of continuously unfolded personas. On Facebook, these are called accounts, and it is the pooling of all accounts that constitute the value of the software because these accounts signal to its advertising clients that there may be precious attention, freely given, to view ads on the platform. As noted, it is these accounts that entrench the positions of companies like Facebook, making it extremely difficult for advertisers and users alike to pursue other options.

Social media companies do not produce content, but harvest, curate, and extract it from users who are tasked with producing selves, giving updates on their lives, displaying feelings, choosing from the 56 available gender identifications offered by the interface's drop-down menu, and the like. The product is deeply enriched, or perhaps is even nothing at all, without its user base actively creating and recreating its intrigue. Therefore, rhetoric that conceptualizes social media platforms as consumer products is misleading in that it leave out the productive dimension and the reliance of the platform's functioning on its base of users. Far from being subversive or oppositional, a minimum of transgressive preferences and odd tastes that break away from media-constructed norms, feeding ever more intensive personalization of services, drives its self-renewal. An epistemology centered on embodied anxiety, hyperactivity, ludicity, compulsivity, and dread become the complex and contradictory terrain upon which compulsive self-performance may waiver back and forth between hyper-inflation and hyper-deflation.

This new regime of digital signification entails front and back ends that demarcate the visible and the invisible of the platform's operations for users. It is no secret that Facebook sells this exposure to users and groups. The monetization of the visibility of posts and other advertising mechanisms create invisible hierarchies of visibility. However, it is difficult to put a price tag on getting a complete grasp of the data traces associated with one's name or accounts. Many have pointed out that even attempting to represent the entities and the procedures that tracking daily activities, locations, and browsing information is a waste of time; too difficult in the state of multilateral, just-in-time surveillance that exists today (see Lovink, 2011; Vaidhyanathan, 2012). There is no neatly collected list of possibilities for modes of capture, simply because there is no oversight that requires it (Pasquale, 2015).

The process of producing self-representing statements that communicate something of users comprises conscious activity on the platform, which obfuscates the modulation and control processes that operate on and link dividuals, as data, behind the scenes. It is along these lines that social subjection and machinic enslavement play off each other to produce the alienating effects of a knowledge that is making important decisions about the user which are not known to it as such. In important ways, the subject must represent itself, but it also does not speak. Sense-making as a practice is displaced to the empirical network overview contained in the proprietary social graph and the flight of its data across multiple agents. Above and below the level of the input of content, of meta-data and deep data, respectively, users are expressed rather than expressing. Facebook registers what is unsaid – clicks, page navigation, hovering used to measure the length of attention, likes, and who we friend are just a few examples. When pictures are uploaded to the site, they are tagged with linguistic descriptors, speaking on behalf of users, by Facebook's recognition algorithms.

The mother lode of the participatory web is identifying habits, relations, and networks of relationships from which can be discerned subjective states of user-groups, like fear or belonging. These account for attentive behaviors and create feedback loops through which users and algorithms turn data into higher-order reflections, rationalizations, and data-driven deployments. In other words, network production is not only a joyous connecting of all-to-all but a system of strong profiling given over to indeterminate operations of those in positions of power and ownership. It is not only users who get to create strong self-representations; owners of data are also free to make art out of the lives of users. Reading the terms of conditions for Facebook, one finds that these data are held on private servers in perpetuity.

The collection of user data, a process that makes itself only barely known and even less understood by users, emanates from the pole of preconscious, class-based interest, as opposed to the schizoid flows of libidinal investment that it charts. This nevertheless has far-reaching effects on subjectification because, in addition to encountering alterity to other users online, the user also encounters alterity to its own subjectivity constructed from above and below, as it were, rendered through the content and sequencing of advertisements, suggestions, user-generated content, and its flow. While the environment of the platform is standardized to a degree, what appears in, say, our news feeds and story suggestions are produced through feedback loops that integrate semiotic, signifying signs produced intentionally and a-signifying signs collected through the mute motions, engagements, and behaviors of users. The flow of content that creates the set and setting of the social space of Facebook comes from our previous acts of clicking, hovering, "checking in" to physical locations, "liking," etc. It is as if the linear past dissolves in the intensification of the present to create an ordered, coherent, and personal informational world.

Because these signs, symbols, and aesthetic blocks are articulated by the machinations of the social graph, they are in some sense deployed by humans and administered through the mediation of artificial intelligence. They come to construct the world available to the user, informing and conditioning its possible social encounters. All the while, undifferentiated digital data become the source of informative metadata that is processed and delivered into the productive sphere. Metadata generated by our engagement with signs, symbols, and aesthetic blocks on the screen contribute to an improved understanding of the demographics-based desire for a range of social purposes, like access to or denial of health care, employment, financial services, and even the allocation of public resources. The ways that individuality and dividuality are played off of each other are contingent and emergent because the degree to which users create their likeness (and stand to have that creation exploited) depends on relations between users and between users and the platform's existing reciprocity and data-sharing agreements and partnerships. They are messy processes whose description can highlight the exploitation and control of individuals through integration with dividuality; the social capacity and technological advances unleashed by the rise of dividual data bodies; and how such in-mixing is what makes Internet technology not a neutral tool, but a highly potent one for those who can leverage such in-mixing to their advantage.

The mapping processes that constitute the social graph described above, and the many ways in which identifications afford new aesthetic and ethical becoming and archaisms comprise our dividuality. All the while, algorithmically informed approximations of us, in the form of packets of information from our browsing, clicking, and managing of on-line features, combine ineffable aspects of subjectivity mapped on to consumption-oriented "user segment" categories. As far as such information is meant to measure the attention and engagement of the subject, it also presumes to link desire to identities. Just like the psy-industrial brand of surveillance for the pathologized, commonly used algorithms employ an epistemology of behavioral and a-signifying signs over linguistic ones, driving a wedge between desiring-production and desire as information about the subject. Social media companies tend to be even less interested in the content users generate between each other than in predicting and tracking user behavior as part of a general mass of all users - this is an ensnaring part of our enculturated habit of self-identity; the paranoia that it generates. The reactionary pole of the user comprises this sort of narcissistic obsession with indiscriminate anonymity, which often comes at the price of minimized participation or walling off, scrambling, and encrypting one side of a bi- or multilateral interaction.

The relational factory

While social relations are deterritorialized and scrambled by capital, externalized memory and communications are produced as a byproduct. These products taken together become fodder for a new, transcendental-structural theory whereby the operations of the algorithm, treated like a new-age god that confers upon users' affects of timelessness, speed, or lost time, enables the partial outsourcing of explorations of the unconscious. Upon the rise of cyberspace in the '90s, theorists like Zizek (1997; 1999) and others took for granted the postmodernist discourse to discuss how "authority" has vanished today, that we are no longer asked to believe in grand narratives or in the submission of the self to the greater good. And yet, nothing could be farther from the case in the age of algorithmic submission; the difference lies exclusively in the fact that the sovereign power of automated, fixed capital is faceless and non-narrative, and thus cannot be reasoned with or appealed to directly. The binding power of the voice is displaced across multi-media alerts, pop-ups, and surprises that command attention. As a proprietary registration machine, social media creates a reliable locus of the attribution of authority; it offers a way of shirking the human relations that it mediates. Authority may be hiding somewhere in the nexuses between humans occupying different ranks in the stratification of the digital social body and computers but rest assured that it is there all the same. That this force of registration is on overdrive, and that we gain only fleeting awareness of this fact, creates an uneasy pact of disdainful submission to the everywhere and nowhere gaseous force of control. Enunciation is undercut in the direct connection between devices and bodies as well as in the force of automation and suggestion that speak in our stead.

The Italian, autonomist Marxist notions of the social factory and their reinterpretation of the general intellect are key here. Perhaps surprising considering their strong emphasis on the power of the worker in overturning their own oppression by capital, the radical thesis of Marx's early "Fragment on Machines" they amplify is that in this machinic "automaton" or "organism" it is no longer the distinct individual entities of the productive workers that are useful for capitalist production, nor even their "work" in a conventional sense of the word, but the whole ensemble of sciences, languages, knowledge, activities, and skills that circulate through a society that Marx (1993) seeks to describe with the terms general intellect (p. 706), social brain (p. 694), and social individual (p. 705). Labor no longer appears to be included directly in the production process; rather, humans as users come to relate more as watchman and regulator to the production process. The absorption of social knowledge and social life into the fixed capital of Facebook's IP and numerous patents indicate that these social facets are direct forces of production.

Algorithms are the mathematical processes that make it possible for machines to improve their performance through learning. They are used for several related purposes, such as automating and rapidly executing repetitive tasks, making comparisons, evaluations, predictions, and novel discoveries within data sets. Algorithms lay out a series of steps by which particular tasks that operate on data and computational structures are to be accomplished (Fuller, 2008). Owing to their agnosticism about the data and the social purpose of the software which they partially comprise, algorithms are abstract processes that exist independently of particular implementations of tasks under specific conditions. While algorithms operate at the moment of necessity, they, like laws, designate the smoothest path of the execution of preprogrammed social values by adjudicating over variations (i.e. new data). The rise of the participatory web 2.0 was also the rise of "big data," creating fine-grained and nuanced bastions of user data for training algorithms. Here we are focusing on Facebook feed content, though one should also be aware that these determine Google search results, Spotify recommendations, and the advertisements, and for that matter, the majority of what one "spontaneously" discovers online.

Facebook's algorithms are the special sauce that makes the company an exclusive curator of digital, social life. Edgerank, the premiere algorithm that operates atop its social graph, directly enables Facebook to bestow this title unto itself. It is the company's version of fixed capital. Recall from Marx's "Fragment" that the creation of the value of machines is always dependent on and presupposes a mass of workers, or in the case of social media, in the age of cybernetic capital, a mass of human beings *as* human beings. However, in addition to the fact that the mass of humans whose additive exuberance creates the value of the platform, this algorithm and its implicit biases make the rules of the platform opaque and mysterious. Extending the notion of the social factory to its micro-targeted control processes, Facebook's algorithm controls visibility (what is seen) and meta-visibility (who or what is seeing this seeing) in the network, making it an effective deterrent of user self-organizing.

Users as human beings, but in their potential as paid workers, are integrated into systems that appropriate their desire as knowledge. Not just in the form of highly discriminatory censorship (because non-romance languages are less well-understood by its algorithms), but also as user data analytics facilitates the automation of industrial, transport, and office work, as well as journalism, translation, law, photography, and other artistic production (Dyer-Witheford, 2015). It would seem that we are not working so much as dedicating ourselves to the development of fixed capital which accelerates the circulation of goods and services necessary for survival and sustenance as if we are all scientists, artists, or academics contributing to the social brain that enables commodities to circulate faster and faster. And yet, this is a generous framing of social media dwellers who are more like Marx's "lumpenproletariat", or even surplus population fighting for relevance. Berardi's (2009) interpretation of the social factory is not that a general intellect a la the collaborative nature of the sciences is the source of value in production, but that the soul is put to work. By this, he means that our attachments, attractions, and inclinations are put to work. Following Deleuze and Guattari, the work of the soul highlights the affective and libidinal nature of productive force over intellectual operations. Though this is something of a false dichotomy along the lines of the well-worn "reasons versus emotions" trope, it is invaluable to point out that the social factory is where these attachments are tested, tried, re-oriented, and modulated.

Capitalist markets here produce subjects, not simply as consumers, but as selves who can be targeted with exacting precision by advertisements but also by various other social opportunities and roles within globally connected markets. This is not only the reproduction of a consumer, as in the industrial era's theory of consumption, which states that capitalism must balance itself by ensuring that workers have sufficient money to be able to buy what they make (or at least survive) on the market. This is a production of selves-as-selves, in a generalized regime of selves-management that navigates a field of overlapping, semi-coincident identifications. Because Facebook operates before the level of production of physical goods and services, it creates identifications that aspire to new lifestyles and expressions. Its competitive attentional landscape is underwritten by an ontology of advertising. The dizzying flight of digital flows and currents, along with the subject's participatory self-management, become fused to industrial and manufacturing processes. Such processes become increasingly driven by the speculative vehicles of predictive data analytics and financial derivatives. While we have focused on an explicit, self-proclaimed social network, the excessive use of the Internet means that the uneven spread of these processes applies in administrative, coordinating, intellectual, manual, industrial, agricultural, and service labor. All these sectors, virtually all human activity, is now overseen and strategically coordinated by continuous electronic surveillance and ongoing analyses of the performance of subjects (Holmes, 2003).

The coding capacity of the computational machines that facilitate the movement of capital, language, and flows of material and immaterial resources transform exchange, making it possible to trade digital assets more and more quickly with less and less a relationship to the material, industrial, and energy production. In the progression of communication infrastructures, digital signs are registered almost simultaneously to their production. As a capacity of the infrastructure of the Internet, this unleashed flow of data affects processes of production, as well as the parthuman effort takes in relation to it. The premium put on collection and extraction of user data, then, coincides with the fall of clock time and the binary configurations that it upheld. Surplus value is not only produced by our forms of employment, sectioned as they are by roles with fixed spatial and temporal coordinates, but by integrating networked computing machines into social life such that value is created from chatting, planning, exchanging, convening, advice-giving, etc. — activities that are not apparently exploitative (Deleuze & Guattari, 1987).

Where capitalism has always sought to extract surplus value from labor in the form of time spent "on the clock," it now seeks to appropriate and extract value from subjective states, experiences, feelings, and social exchange. As this form of social labor spreads across the day, existing as "flow and circulation within time" and comprising "the relation between production time and reproduction time, as a single whole" — capital aims to impose time-as-measure against "the conception of working-class freedom over the temporal span of life" (Negri, 2003a, pp. 89–91). This happens through an opaque system of measurement, facilitated by the use of digital information technologies, that extract surplus value on a machinic temporality that is not confined to a time or space that would otherwise designate "labor" or "leisure" for a new, precarious group of users. That this intensive, machinic temporality is *all the time* gives rise to, for instance, YouTube cultural commentary that prefaces a two-year-old memory by signaling awareness that two years is like a hundred years in Internet time (see Wynn, 2019).

The rise of self-marketing, branding, and the influencer economy make it easy to qualify Facebook as a type of social labor. Yet, at a step of removal from the prospect of successful self-advertising, are the complex ethical and valuating decisions made on these platforms. Secretly in service to the social proficiency of proprietary algorithms, users mark out what they believe is real by contributing to aesthetic blocks and digital objects and texts. By operating at this degree of removal from the meager, ultra-competitive "empowerment" afforded by the loudspeaker of social media, such value production is disqualified from recognition as labor in the traditional sense. This disqualification reflects the false binary of production and consumption along the lines of a paid and unpaid dichotomy. As we have emphasized, the environment of the platform relies on the social imagination and desiring of users, despite the degree of over-determination of its actions. Profits are generated from the differently manifested but overarching maintenance of social ties – the concrete manifestations of care, but also of anxiety, of the imagined social totality.

Digital archives, in the case of Facebook and its patented social graph, are integrated, through machine learning, back into these algorithms so that they improve themselves (i.e., increase their ability to provide what we want to see). Put simply, this knowledge is a barreling, ongoing process rather than a static set of facts. Like all other computer-based "calculational" media, archives are falsely characterized as "things" because, in contrast with traditional archives that couple with cultural memory, digital archives have no intrinsic macro-temporal index (as the Y2K bug scare demonstrated; Ernst, 2013). They operate at a micro-temporal level. In fact, Facebook's graph changes so quickly that any moment of retrieval is but a snapshot of the dynamics of the ongoing process of data collection and aggregation. The archive gives way to archival dynamics and its control structures rather than the specifics of its contents. Its primary operations, then, are not sorting the content of files, but their linkages, just as the Web is defined by its protocols (HTTP, TCP/IP) rather than what one may or may not find there.

Marx's *Fragments* also suggests that the "alien" power of the algorithm is a stop late in the march of autonomous machines, shifting conditions of labor such that machinic processes appropriate and embed the knowledge of human beings, but also such that the machine comes to be identified with increasingly fixed conditions that delimit how and why work must be done. The commonality between machines and laws is that they are both formal embodiments of the relative automation of actions and decisions. In law, this operates through precedent, codification, and conventions of interpretation. When law evolves, it takes precedent into account by attempting to circumscribe and codify possible future variations on past events to reduce operational friction in the reproduction of accumulated social values.

It is important to mention here that there are also humans who labor as aids to the Edgerank and Facebook's other steering algorithms. The labor of "ethics," or realistically, reproducing a vision of civil society, falls to content moderators who repress for us whatever does not adhere to Facebook's "community standards." These standards are molded to the profitability of Facebook, maintained by its paid wage laborers, and subject to change without notice. As Facebook and other social media are increasingly held up to public scrutiny, their community standards become targets of outrage and dispute. Those formally employed by Facebook also face precarization, in that it is solely a question of executive judgment as to whether or not cognitive labor like moderating, analyzing, and even writing content is delegated to its algorithms instead. It is only a matter of time before exhaustion with human messiness and clever means of eschewing responsibility for important management decisions will make trusting algorithms rather than humans a safer bet for the company.

As a corporation, Facebook prefers to hide behind the same technological force that also mystifies users: its algorithms. More and more, though, its adjudication of user reach, visibility, and censorship reaches popular awareness. The network effects that empowers the ultra-popular hubs and ultra-connected users can also be superseded by outright censorship when it wields a sort of the despotic power to delete content and accounts with little or no explanation. Recently, Facebook has come under scrutiny for deactivating and censoring grassroots movements and activists, especially from the Arab world, while claiming that it has no right to censor the speech of political officials - even when these do not conform to their community standards.

The social web combines machine and law-like codifications because semiotic-machinic processes operate on presumed completeness of knowledge, decidedly out of the grasp of human beings; it is the social body in its infinite unfolding, recursively in response to itself. As Marx (1990, p. 694) famously noted of machinery, the value objectified therein "appears as a presupposition against which the value-creating power of the individual labor capacity is an infinitesimal, vanishing magnitude." This notion subtends the alienation of producer and product, or producer and use-value, he ascribed to mass production. The machinery keeps absorbing the accumulation of knowledge and skill that should belong to labor; in other words, it helps wins the competition between labor and capital for the "general productive forces of the social brain." While possession of the social brain, like language, is formally impossible, control over its flows is the proper locus of the struggle for the procedures and protocols that inscribe subjectivity. That social networks come to represent this all-absorbing, nonhuman (or trans-human) wealth of knowledge, a sort of empirical science of social relations that nobody can have, makes the gaps between data, information, and knowledge equally the site of the contested production of value in the digital economy.

The relational factories of social media provoke and capitalize individualized becoming such that they can be re-territorialized on individual identities behind the scenes. Note that we users all capitalize some on our individual identities, making the stratification of the digital social body presented here not absolute, but conceptual and productive. We selectively lock up bits of information, modulate its flow, share this and not that, and capitalize to varying degrees on our unfounded, "claimed" privations of collective linguistic and semiotic stock. Nevertheless, all of this is properly owned by Facebook, which enables it to apply predictive analytics that use elements of actual on-line activity as well as demographic norms from statistical aggregates to presume and predict this user or user group's behavior. This progressively creates a social network of ambient and perpetual suggestion. Data doubles are "us" as "epistemic objects" (or to put it less academically, stereotypes) mediated by categorical sorting and analysis, through a variety of probabilistic calculations. Our data create shadow profiles of us that generate individualized on-line affordances through a credit-score like a system of offerings that arise on the basis of our likelihood of, not even purchasing but engaging with, this or that idea.

Further, users are segmented toward the determination of their eligibility for social-institutions-turned-services, like healthcare, education, and credit. The linking and modeling of users become yet another way that discrimination is systematized behind the scenes. The automated flow of data also has unpredictable ramifications for off-line communities linked through economic circuits informed by this data. When I buy a backpack on Facebook's (official) marketplace, for example, I have no idea whether or not the data they purchase produced will be aggregated in a set used to predict the likelihood of educational success in my region. If convincing to the relevant governing and funding institutions, this data means a massive influx or outflow of capital and other materials that could affect youth quality of life, crime rates, etc. In this case, algorithmic patterns are referred to as interpretation whose methods are opaque to the users and the groups into which they are unknowingly and perhaps unwittingly sorted.

Data streams (dividuality/enslavement) linked with self-nominations (individuality/subjection) come to impact life in a variety of ways. Our dividuality, therefore, becomes both our past and our future – not to mention that privately funded initiatives of all sorts are justified on the basis of social data that is the aggregation of all of this individual user data. For users, as much as for society, operationalized as a collection of individuals, the past that diminishes in the rapidity of the computing experience returns, filtered through predictions. It works the other way, too, from off-line to on-line. For instance, a visit to the doctor's office that results in a drug-store purchase of ibuprofen might be exchanged as data with a company whose ad appears on your Facebook feed, collated with your indicated interest in trail-running, for a "healthier alternative for pain management." As a group of individuals and as a networked collective of Facebook users, we are predicted in advance but also interpreted with effects that sputter out into the future. Algorithmic interpretation of our online behavior sees patterns of engagement rather than meaning. For instance, if one incidentally stumbles upon child pornography, the metadata of this engagement trajectory does not register moral outrage, shame, or guilt, but it does mark this fact of the matter, along with the IP address that provides the means of locating the user in physical time-space. As Jarod Lanier explains in *Welcome to the Machine* (Anderson et al., 2012), any profit-driven predictive system must be just better than competitors' predictions, but not right all the time.

Social mapping as value production: Part two

Value in the digital economy emerges not only from the lost time of individuals – a measure of control like what we saw in psychology's addiction construct, but from the formalization and commodification of their affective relations and affiliations. Looking at this process in detail is informative. The rapidly obsolescent and ultra-transparent selves created online are subject to user-wide statistical aggregation and categorized on the basis of the data brokers or advertisers' imagined communities. Usually, these imagined communities are formed around measurements of your interests – insofar as these interests inform your brand loyalties, buying habits, creditworthiness, and even social status as measured by your friends' friends and *their* debiting habits. Facebook Beacon was an invention from 2007 – the first user-tracking program that explicitly placed advertisements in users' news feeds based on their friends' behavior. Though Beacon was shut down in 2009, this "friends of friends" flaw has continued up to the present. At the time of writing, Facebook is under scrutiny again when internal emails containing decisions about which other tech companies would be granted access to the "Friends API," which precisely relays these social status metrics.

These are fodder for the creation of social categories that, along with other categories of predictive data, are known as "conventions of interpretation in enabling market rationality and making value decisions possible" (Arvidsson & Colleoni, 2012, p. 141). For example, in the realm of asset classes or finance, these data pieces, in addition to the use of other public data, become the key to the valuation and likelihood of success of various services, commodities, digital technologies, etc. This makes the manipulation of such technologies highly problematic, as it frames and harvests: the types of questions it asks, the forms of communication it facilitates, its design, its regulation, and its business practices all come into play.

Prediction algorithms also assemble group relations, demarcating, and utilizing the social groupings of individual users it creates. These categories do not come from nowhere but embed the values of its "sense-makers" (e.g., the designers and managers who control the software). These categories amplify divisions and distinctions *within* the imaginary social groups of its back-end graph. Preferences and predilections are categorized and reinforced through the recycling of user-produced semiotics. Their comings and goings are therefore also timed according to Facebook's impetuses to form strategic partners and sales and to spark more activity. It is not merely that the entire network of users who fill Facebook with interesting content do not have assurances of accessibility to what they produce, nor control of its distribution (unless they buy advertising which marginally pumps up the volume of the message they wish to spread), nor editing rights. It is that these users are regrouped and affiliated ("matched") by methods unknown to them.

If the interplay between individuality and dividuality creates a data "doubles" as placeholders for all users, this same effect occurs for groups of users. The full force of network capitalization is derived from the strength *between* relationships and groups determined through bubbles of hype around particular commodities, brands, experiences, political ideologies, and other identifications. While this particular exploration is outside the scope of this piece, social media may in truth offer a direct demonstration of the linkage between marginalized identities and identifications, and of connection between class struggle and liberal identity political categories. This is because Facebook's social graph is valuable as a digital asset for its ability to trace large movements of human sentiment through associations. While this is obvious insofar as it sells data analytic services to its clients, Facebook owns experimental initiatives, like its non-consensual and unauthorized Emotional Manipulation (or sometimes Contagion) Study attests to its willingness to play with users to prove its influence and might (Flick, 2016). Value expands, not strictly through the production of commodities, but by the mechanisms through which they circulate through the lives that foreground them. Voyeuristic and exhibitionist preparations of bloated selves create a social link built on the ontology of advertising that creates users who appear to desire "the new" per se, which is also to say, nothing in particular.

The status of knowledge embodied in the social graph is one of the habitual sets of relations; not what we like, or even what we do, but the sets of relations between entities, acts, and people. The associations between users as dividuals, personified to each other through accounts, are taken at face(less) value. In the market analyses made possible by the social graph, frequency and proximity displace meaning. Words index communication by the fact that they appear, representing relations devoid of content. At root, the value of the social graph is precisely the visibility of the private relationships between users, with a speculative price for how much these people's business is worth to advertisers and companies competing for consumers at a time of decreasing spending power of the masses. Subjection (individual) and enslavement (dividual) does not refer just to differential exercises of power upon discrete persons but of social organization. The same operation that plays these figures of human wholeness and reduction to a mass of data off of each other therefore scales up. This creates groups of individuals in conscious connection, through affiliation, whose coming together is interpersonal, and (quasi, or potential) collectives of dividuals whose symbolic linkage as nodes in the network is inter-subjective, and which creates the value of the platform.

The argument here is that the connection "between people" of Facebook is one that already empties out in advance the mutative possibilities of expression by re-coding them in its graph via the account of the individual so preserved. Facebook is positioned as a sort of central planning agency for such connective recoding, raising the stakes of association in its perpetual inscription and selective sharing with other social web companies. The ultra- formalized and exposed selves created online are subject to user-wide statistical aggregation, formed around measurements of interests – insofar as these interests inform our brand loyalties, buying habits, creditworthiness, even as measured by our friends' friends and *their* debiting habits, for example.

Meanwhile, groups are consciously forged through relations of "liking" informational objects of identification. On Facebook, one may accept an invitation to, or request to join, a group, say, "Dog Lovers." In this group, there are administrators and particular community rules (e.g., "members may post once a day to ease the number of posts" or "members may only post pictures of their own dogs"). The group is organized from above based on its inclusion into rather than distinction from the algorithmic curation of the platform. Such groups are part of a mechanism of categorization, or a convention of interpretation (coding) that tether onto individual accounts.

Sometimes hailed as governance playgrounds, groups catch users in their guise as whole persons in social microcosms or digital town squares. Groups are veritable playgrounds in that they are practice spaces for following and perhaps even making rules about the conduct of interaction, what one intentionally displays, etc. Such consensual (conscious) spaces of (inter)action are treasure troves for any social science researcher, advertiser, or government agency specializing in citizen surveillance.

The introduction of social buttons allows for objectification and valorization not of the time spent by users on-line, but of their ability to create webs of affective attachments around informational objects. Such objects are valued according to their ability to move affect, sometimes called their network centrality (Gerlitz & Helmond, 2011). Repetition produces value in network production in that it creates the appearance of stability in a leaky and transient world of digital signals (Chun, 2016). Informational events must be repeated such that they can continue to exist at a micro-temporal scale. It becomes valuable upon its move from a singularly noted event to one that elicits a response en masse. It is in this sense that the generated value does not depend on the particular individual but on the interconnections between the engagement of a collection of individuals-dividuals. Outside of the collaborative nature of knowledge itself, which involves the collective effects of voluntary actions, "the value of information emerges through the involuntary effects of voluntary and involuntary actions, from like searches, likes, posts, and mouse clicks" (*ibid*, p. 119). And, while they may organize themselves, groups are ontologically indistinct from users and other informational objects. According to the social graph protocol, they are yet more virtual objects to be inscribed (Hui & Halpin, 2013). What groups miss, even as they become more censorious or implement high barriers of entry, is an accounting of their own structural limitations. Groups do not touch the temporal modulation owing to the structure of Facebook, its software, its governance, its profits, and the sets of material and social relations they mold and perpetuate.

Records are exchanged that approximate (but inherently cannot target) something like user intentionality, making users markers in social models that speak for them. Currently, users have the least agency in the hierarchy of builders, executives, operators, consumers, and raw materials in the digital economy. The maps that they build are not accessible, editable, or contestable by them, even as they may affect their lives in numerous ways. Neither do they have access to the value they create. The rights to record, to formulate categories, to deploy data sets for a range of social-engineering purposes, and to otherwise realize accounts (data) as surplus value is created in the setting up of the infrastructure for the circulation of these accounts and relevant pieces of data that pertain to, and emanate from them. It is in this sense that changes in the evolution of capital's de- and re-coding process designates shifts in its style and capacity to dominate subjects. Wendy Brown (2006) argues that the innovations in forms of control translate genealogical attachments and identifications into right, which could not be better exemplified here. All the way back in 2006, Facebook's trademark was granted, and its intellectual property, the social graph, protected. In fact, Facebook holds some seven to eight thousand patents for data mining of tags, keywords, and user-attentional and behavioral patterns. The share of users, then, is nothing more than the spontaneous investment (creation) of self or selves, incarnated digitally in bodies of personal data.

7
CONCLUSION

A proposal to psychologists

Our collective migration in the wake of digital imperialism and the creation of the "social factory" of social media are of a piece with each other. Our participation in social media networks is a condition of survival in today's capitalism. It is part of an apparatus of capture, with its characteristic maneuvers of "expansion, propagation, occupation, contagion, peopling" (Deleuze & Guattari, 1987, p. 239). The apparatus of capture of social media is, at first, a form of forced migration. It gets everyone on the platform. This assures that there is someone that everyone cares about on social media.

Social life increasingly becomes infused with capitalism; social relations are directly productive, and yet they do not describe the capitalist relations of production that realize its massive value as money. Commercialization of the Internet and the emergence of networked, distributed production give rise to many new forms of organization for changing the dynamics of power in society. The vectoralist fight to stay in control of the circulation of information also involves severely limiting the autonomy of the many to enrich themselves and those around them at little cost. I have attempted to describe these relations philosophically, geographically diffuse, disguised, and faceless as they may be.

I propose that psychologists contribute a human-centered unification of Internet-age problems recognized in piecemeal fashion by the likes of the WHO, most countries' legal systems, journalists, pundits, and others. The haphazard adaptation of addiction disorders to a range of modern phenomena, of which Internet and Social Media Addictions are a part are what psychologists have contributed thus far. This has spread a highly intelligible trope, providing a language for the widespread recognition of a shift in the texture of daily life and individuals' visceral dependence on digital technologies. Yet, it remains the case that the addiction trope in psychology has and will continue to serve the psy-industrial purpose of singling out individual extreme cases for submission to techniques of behavioral control vis-a-vis digital networks.

The current individualistic approaches to net politics mirror this by focusing on privacy and security – these approaches are unable to address the relational creation of surplus-value. As this examination of social media platforms relayed, the commodification of selves turns out to also require the commodification of affective relations and social affiliations. The knowledge embodied in social media software is one of the habitual sets of relations between entities, acts, and users. The collective nature of excessive net use is built into the technical architecture of platforms and the power laws of networks to which they give rise, making the individualization of harm in response incomplete and somewhat banal. The opportunity to pivot from understanding individuals, alone to toil with their agency as a consumer of pre-given online services that they use to connect across time and space, to users as a collective with agency proper to this whole group, is upon us.

While evidence for the specific effects of the Internet and social media use is thin, the conviction that it is problematic pours over with passion. While we wait with bated breath for scientific confirmation of our suspicions about problems like "continuous partial attention" (e.g., Firat, 2013), neurological deficits from excessive screen time (Davis et al., 2019), deregulation of biorhythms (Crary, 2013), the limitations of social awareness and meta-cognitive failures imposed by over-reliance on audio-visual cues (Varakin, et al., 2004), and other hypothesized specific effects, there is an opportunity to shift the balance of power online to extend the social benefits of social media. Again, it is this balance of power that I have suggested is the root cause of the sad effects of addiction: dependence, powerlessness, and loss of control, and its incentivization of extreme and evocative modes of participation and exclusion that condition anger, hate, and jealousy.

Users, taken as a collective base, lack of control over their externalized memory. Users go about performing themselves on social media, and this performance is never complete. It is continually disrupted by algorithmically induced suggestions for additions to assemblages of subjectivity, some of which stick, but many of which dissolve rapidly into the social web's massive stock of semiotic materials. I suggest that the design of social media like Facebook short-circuits a continuity of the development of subjectivity that has the effect of returning users over and over again to a sort of existential "ground zero". Users, the digital, social "we", precariously navigate the trendy terrain of quickly evolving prompts and directives for self-performance, all the while lacking a deep understanding of the ramifications of their formalization and use. Both the power of suggestion and the powerful analytic tools that see the whole view of a person in context is reserved exclusively for vectoralists and their software engineering henchmen. This power is used commercially but is also reinvested in platforms to build even more compelling means of self-performance in ever shorter loops, with the overall result of keeping users locked into and dependent on the platform itself.

The formation of subjective and existential territories, particularly individualizing ones, is the business of social media companies and psychologists alike. This brings us to the role of psychologists in the digital social body. Very generally speaking, psychology, with its interpretive frames and its parameters of normality and pathology and its modulation thereof, offers an intimate, "analog" version of many of the cultural processes now dominated by social media. The very possibility that the Internet can be understood as an object of addiction could be rooted in this situatedness, which understandably involves a fear of losing jobs to tele-therapists or becoming tele-therapists, undermining their training and practices, or even having the practice of therapy slowly automated by software in the same way that even the most sophisticated forms of neuroscience, not to mention its less philosophically savvy iterations, threaten theoretical and philosophical psychology. If psychology is aware of its own situatedness within the regime of cybernetic capitalism in this way, it stands to both improve its recommendations around Internet use as a decisive locus of social justice and material remediation of psycho-social ills beyond the individual.

Marxist scholar David Harvey (2018) notes that it took quite a while and a lot of experience before the proletariat learned to distinguish between machinery and its employment by capital, and therefore to transfer their attacks from the material instruments of production to the form of society which utilizes those instruments. Psychologists should take heed, also because the externalization of memory online, the upload to corporate servers that constitutes the self-performance practice of using social media for users, has significant crossover with the talking cure and the glimpses of the unconscious it reveals. While social media uses an incredible variety of semiotic material for subjectivation, it shares the strange intimacy of knowing exposure to a faceless other that Lacan (2007) might have understood in connection with his "discourse of the analyst". Think about the use of a simple search: the authoritative bearer of answers is occupied by the platform's algorithmic knowledge. The maintenance of this position, in the analyst's discourse, structures the transference between analyst and analysand. In like fashion, the fetishism of the platform's algorithmic knowledge and its linkage with a sweeping body of folk knowledge, a treasure trove of linguistic and semiotic material that is always being written, supports an ominous sense of asymmetrical knowledge/power whereby the user is given over to the truth of the incompleteness or unsatisfactory nature of knowledge.

Yet, users are subjects of digital signifiers as data. This is a distinctive position from the psychoanalytic subject of linguistic signifiers and speech, though subjection to linguistic signifiers obviously does not stop but is morphed in relation to processes of digitization. As a phase in the mechanist evolution of technics, cybernetic self-reference and reflexivity apply to an ontogenetic process that informs the coming-to-be of individuals and institutes trans-individual relations – relations that affect material and conceptual syntheses of individuality and collectivity. The Internet (im) materializes a passage from language to the neutralization of sense, to a-semiotic intensity as data. This part of the passage is key to value production in the digital age. Data is desire, which is crucially different from speech requisite for healing, democracy, and civilization as we know it. The schizoanalytic unconscious is additive rather than substitutive, making users speaking subjects and subjects of a-signifying, digital data that are shards and fragments of disperse desire that is sometimes delivered back to the realm of significance and interpretation but is most often shuttled through automatic, pre-programmed processes where they are waste, never to be seen again, or component parts of decisions made without users' consent. We are beat to the punch, so to speak when it comes to the purposes to which our names, words, and data traces are put. Reclaiming data as such, and as a social, artistic, and political raw material for self-reference, is a crucial site of struggle for the autonomous production of subjectivity today.

If the role of psychologists is at least partly to facilitate some form of subjectivation and self-reflexiveness in the context of another person's life, then psychologists should view social media moguls as their true competitors in the digital social body. I propose here the development of analog and digital tools to amplify coordinates of subjectivation, to create a space specifically designed as complementary and adjacent to the cramped spaces of social media, to explore with more slowness and less pressure the affects and selfhood developed on social platforms, and to investigate the specific difficulties of users *as users*. As it stands now, it seems that psychologists are not terribly disposed to deep pedagogy on the basis of one's online activity, neither in terms of social power, as here, nor any other imaginable meaning.

Reducing behaviors to quantities of use (hours piddled away being jealous of others on social media, for example) simply bolsters the false binary between the real, physical world and the ideal, digital world without noticing how these worlds inform each other so quickly and powerfully that understanding them separately is quickly becoming counterproductive. One need only think of the fiber optic cables running through the ground and the seas to connect us via the Internet, or the fact that the Internet uses more than 10% of the energy in the world – a figure which is expected to rise beyond the amount of renewable energy it is currently possible to produce.

Desire

We have seen how, for Deleuze and Guattari, desire produces the real in and of itself, but not as the pursuit of a goal or a completed intention. Desire is productive precisely because it veers from its own course, is not natural or given, and surprises us with its own decay (Tuck, 2010). It is a process of interaction of heterogeneous elements whose combinations and permutations are not given in advance and do not fit neatly into particular structures that would finalize our understanding of it once and for all. It is plainly given in the way that value is produced in the digital economy that this is precisely what is exploited by platform vectoralists and their clients. In the framework of the increasing refinement from data, to information, and even knowledge, it is *knowledge* that is the least subject to enclosure. While data is tucked away behind the scenes and information its statistical, computational output, knowledge affords something different, but what?

I suggest that what is possible here is not an interpretive knowledge, as that which is produced in the wielding of analytic power conferred in access to data and information. The knowledge that comes into play here is instead knowledge of desire itself, in its shirking from nominalism and its lack of fixity. Desire is the force that plays the game of resisting oppression against all appearances. It is not that desire desires revolution explicitly, but that its very nature causes derailments and displacements in the social fabric (Deleuze, 2004). It is the cause of power's organization, not the result of it. It is mostly unconscious, but it is by no means dumb or base. Rather, it is strategic and cunning, only revealing itself in moments of dire necessity. It is this knowledge and this analysis, that desire does not need healing, fixing, or interpreting, which is the least appreciated in a globalizing culture dominated by techno- and pharmaco-solutionism.

The notion of desire applies vividly to the imagination of a social totality demonstrated in the contradictions, context-mashing, and constructions of user selfhood. Desire invests the social field surprisingly indiscriminately, making the half-century-old Deleuzo-Guattarian declarations about extra-familial investments seem almost parochial. This hypertext is the fantastical "All" of the global socius of users, or the whole world of knowledge, people, experiences, and life – the perpetual "out there" of the new, the intensive "just for us", and the affective encounters with alterity which the online world holds as an implicit promise. The users' role is to generate signifiers and data traces, from their innumerable encounters with alterity in the cramped spaces of corporate social media. Just as Facebook automatically creates ghost profiles in anticipation of yet-to-be users, anyone can simply start a club, an event, a place, a business page as a beacon, and a frame, without expectation of particular linkages or correspondences to facets of life beyond it. The coming on-line of new fantasy entities that can be placed in connection to other things on Facebook's social graph show that byproducts of speech open onto the realm of the combinatory, additive, and symbolic possible. It is this libidinal, imaginative outpouring which constitutes the abstract labor of digital production and of which societies of control are profoundly generative. It is not the "unreal", but the difficulty of discerning the real and the unreal, given that the distinction between them is in perpetual flux (Deleuze, 1997, p. 66).

The semiotic slide across varying registers of subjective and material, ontological consistency (see especially Deleuze & Parnet, 2007; Guattari, 1995, 2011, 2013) works in tandem with the root fact that social media is an empirical, statistical formalism that operates on the abstract totality, *society at large,* a market which it creates. Facebook and other social media work upon the abstract totality, the placeholder, of the socius itself, insinuating itself into the crisis of subjectivity described by Foucault and Guattari in the early 1980s (Lazarrato, 2014). It becomes a cybernetic science *of* this crisis, massively outshining the social scientific disciplines in its ability to mold and produce subjectivity. Hence the Internet Addiction rhetoric of hijacking of brains, and in extreme cases, apparently trumping in subjective estimation the importance of bodily needs like eating, sleeping, and physical contact with other human beings. As a portal to its formalized world, it offers this social totality as a glimmering lure, which lacks only you and your unique mode of entry. Moreover, as an antidote to this crisis, and the failure of an entrepreneurial subjection modeled on the American bourgeois logic of relationships, it is also a machine for appropriating pre-capitalist archaisms, nationalisms, fascisms, and authoritarianisms. Social media illuminates that these are not only alive and well but require constant warding off and re-coding by capital. De- and re-coding is no metaphor, as humans and machines work together to censor, displace, and make legible that which is useful for capital's maintenance of general engagement or specific enticement.

Bernard Stiegler (1998, 2005) calls this excess, the investment of this whole field, the means of collective individuation. He echoes thinkers like Paolo Virno and Gilbert Simondon, affirming that "the collective" is the condition of possibility for individuation (rather than its deferral, individualization). Thinking individuation rather than individualization draws much-needed attention to the pre- and trans-individual qualities of perception and language. What's important is separating processes of individuation from the creation of individuals as closed-off, political-economic entities that exist, primarily, to reproduce existing hierarchies of social power. Unlike the creation of individuals, the process of psychical and collective individuation is a becoming-other in the presence of the other. In dealing with disorders related to Internet excesses, the role of the psychologist may be to hold space for the proliferation of desire produced between individuals, sensitive to its closure and cooptation by programming constraints and platform mandates "from above" that does not do justice to other, minor desires and proclivities. Counter-intuitively, the assumption that digital platforms give voice to the many covers up the profound foreclosure of users, as a collective, coming to know their desire as active, living force. This happens at the level of "filter bubbles", where news feeds, personalized from historical user data, deliver to the user only intensified and voluminous assertions of their preexisting beliefs and opinions, but also in the technical lock-up of data and the determination of its value as money. Becoming-other, in the Deleuzo-Guattarian, Stieglerian, and Simondonian senses do not imply an aping or mimicking of the other, but learning how to be *with* that is open to the liminality and uncertainty of change in the absence of a need to have become, once and for all.

Collective user-sovereignty

The binding power or performative efficacy of enunciation, in the last instance, is outsourced to the social graph, Edgerank, and other algorithms, under the control of the Facebook corporation. The formation of users is part of the creation of these new social institutions that are singularly motivated by the profit imperative despite appearances and posturing otherwise. The conventional, "target" user is inflected with a sense of neutrality; a generic utilitarianism does not exactly identify the user as a consumer, though this is largely the current use of the massive advertising platforms we call social media. Users are also subjects-to-come for platform designers, delineated as much by the purpose set out for it as how they are used for perceived self-interest (even when this runs awry) (Bratton, 2015). Users' accounts are transactional hubs, the logic of which subordinates anything else represented by this name (e.g., the subject in of communication).

How can we hold for a politics of desire in this landscape, as to meet this creation of linkages between past and future? What we need to reconcile here is the machinic conjunctions of desire's free flow that at times gives rise to assemblages that afford an awareness of how its couplings and connections extend and multiply, coming together in ingenious configurations that we could not have imagined in advance. How can we allow some degree of the autonomy of desire to take the reins, all the while acknowledging that such a declension would be of a piece, too, with human-user self-determination? As we can see in the above analysis of users and vectoralists, social media has the affordance of laying bare the social relation as a relation of asymmetry, involving poles of activity and receptivity and its degrees of freedom. As per a schizoanalytic methodology, a collective self-critique and experimentation with new social forms are possible owing to the technologies developed in concert with processes of capitalist production and appropriation. We must ask if these networks can become agents of reflexivity, and if not, what needs to change so that this can occur?

Concerns about the shape the social net has taken have already generated numerous calls to do things like: re-invent central planning using the mass of user-generated "big data" as more efficient price signals (Phillips & Rozworski, 2019) socialize data centers (Morozov, 2015), make the Internet and social media companies into public utilities with more regulation and better tax compliance, and incite demands for a fully-automated, post-capitalist utopia (Srnicek & Williams, 2016). The contradictions of intellectual property, the cordoning off of knowledge and cultural resources which are not inherently scarce, but can even be considered to become *more valuable* the more people have access and paths to contribute back to them, comes to a tragicomic apex in the digital economy of cybernetic capitalism. The free software, open-source development, and pirate communities, alongside nonprofits and foundations that support and advocate throwing off the shackles of personal property online, have presented too numerous grassroots initiatives to present here. With a keen awareness of how damaging social media and the social web can be, calls for reforms and acts of resistance have increased substantially in the past five years from a murmur in niche communities of thinkers to a roar across fields such as science and technology studies, law, philosophy, digital media studies, cultural studies, and political science.

For the purpose of a critical psychology of users attuned to the importance of the collective as the means of individuation, the production of value on social media platforms is an instance in which the processes of capital accumulation and circulation run up against and substantially devalue processes of social reproduction. The question of excessive use of the Internet gives us the chance to grapple with the irony that the creation of surplus-value today, which Deleuze and Guattari (1987) called machinic surplus value, adapts people to social relations colonized by capital directly. Where monetary surplus is concerned, affective labor on social media produces "selves" as positive externalities. Our subjectivation and their various materials are de-contextualized, dissolved into a veritable ocean of data, and sold or rented out as the platform and its offerings. Whether it is paid or unpaid, considered to be part of work or not to or by the user, value production on social media platforms in their current form involves pricing and thereby also seizing, indirectly, a measure of control over social re-production. Desire, sociality, affect, and care are capitalized on social media platforms. Psychologists should be among those watching with awe as love and care emerges glaringly as crucial to value creation in the era of networks, while labor as such supports *it*.

If we generate value on Facebook so feverishly, to the point at which, for many, such behavior resembles an addiction, it would seem that we already have a large share in the infrastructure of the social graph. The challenge for a constructive politics of the Internet today can go beyond acts of defiance or asceticism in the resistance to the Internet where users renounce online communication, for example, to the tender, pre-digital days of yore. Atop the question of face-to-face or technologically mediated relations sits the question of extractive or non-extractive mediation. The massive wealth and power disparities arising from the elite ownership of a whole collective body of data, a data *commons*, may be remedied through a great experiment in collective ownership and governance of the infrastructure that users co-construct. This would further entail a greater degree of mutuality in the human–software relationship and the human–human relationships they variably magnify and obscure. Is it possible to redress the commodification of relationships without the mediation of the Facebook company's rentier status and predictive social control? This could be done by removing the constraints and design parameters of popular communication media from capital. This *is only possible at the mass level* because of the dynamics of network effects and social lock-in discussed above. Our choice of software, hardware, and Telecomms are our cultural interfaces and constitute a crucial realm of ethics for users. We must invest ourselves in the technological future that we collectively seek, endeavoring for a deeper understanding of the ramifications of our migratory patterns through digital-physical and physical-digital space.

Only be removing the constraints of the profit motive can the value of social media be understood *as social,* with huge consequences for value as money online but also for value as a social benefit *for itself* which stretches far beyond the (re)distribution of money to users and toward total redesign and restructuring. Only a small group of elites and a web of capital commitments decide which technologies develop sufficiently to become exposed. Beyond freeing data-as-data, and monetary value of social media to its true (libidinal) investors, users, there is the development of new tools altogether that more readily conform to what it is users want from distance communication. Among the negative consequences of social media in its current form is the stifling of imagination for the use of information technologies, and the different socio-political universes to which they call.

Holding, maintaining, and using data can be structured to foster engagement like collective, user-governance, and stewardship modeled on cooperatives. Collective ownership and cooperative models could give way to a post-ownership society in which a culture of love for maintaining the means of coordination for the many, an anarchic but organized web, becomes a reality. Collective self-organization is, then, a necessary and missing piece of the puzzle. To this end, one could imagine something like user-permitted socialization of existing data, and the use of social media itself for mass deliberation and negotiation of interface features, and regulatory action regarding the now-conventional use of boilerplate contracts for software and online services. If we are to be able to appreciate and share in the social value, not in the form of money, but in the organization, communication, and planning on the basis of users' data, we must also be able to trust that we will have a certain degree of control over when data is collected at all, or when it might be directed to a sort of digital dump, and where we consent to wholesale monitoring.

Our data bodies and big data are a second- or third-nature commons, the stuff from which new forms of social cooperation might be modeled. One might also imagine what would happen if social media companies opened access to the full stock of its social laboratory and back-end data analytic tools to more established institutions. The social sciences have garnered centuries of related knowledge, distinctly humane and subject-centered methodologies, and ethics learned from many difficult failures that, in hindsight, constituted a collective trauma from which much was duly learned and remains a crucial field of study (e.g., post-colonialism, critical race theory, gender studies). Because the corporatization of online environments is part and parcel of digital imperialism and users' collective migration, dealing with the preservation of data may become a site of collective deliberation and prioritization that susses out interest in data as a collectively produced commons. Narratives created against the backdrop of the ostensibly cold, hard facts of behavioral, attentional, and geospatial data are used to justify, legitimate, and influence all sorts of human decision making and population engineering, so the creation of data-backed narratives have and will continue to be requisite parts of social impact (Ippolita, 2015).

On this line of thought, one gets a glimpse at the possibilities for collective action beyond demanding wages from Facebook (http://wagesforfacebook.com/), or even social media companies' own creation of charitable funds. The modification of individual behavior could eventually be collectivized and democratized to pursue goals, for example, dismantling systemic racism, sexism, and planet destructive growth-oriented economies. Seizing the means of production is not sufficient when it comes to the production of the social *as* the social; we must also re-imagine the relations of production and means of coordination through multiple, shifting sub-collectives of users that grow together or apart on the basis of interest in using data in different ways for projects with connections to other cultural institutions that vary in breadth and reach.

Now, simply being able to access the social groupings arrived at by machine-learning algorithms is a place to start. On most of the platforms that collect the most data about us, like Facebook, data is not only harvested exclusively for marketing, but is also asymmetrically accessible; masses of platform-wide data is sold and circulated, while users are left with their personal data which only lends itself to curation and management of on-line presence – for purposes that do not facilitate cooperative engagement but the enhancement of individuals, like atoms, whose collisions foster anger, jealousy, image-management, and sadness. A genuine alternative would be truly distributed, where no one has privileged access to user data. As collectives, users could class manifold, qualitatively different types of data in the creation of categories that reflect the social interests of specific productive collectives.

Given the collective ontology of the Internet, self-reflexivity dissolves into collective reflexivity (provided there is nothing preventing this). For this reason, "platform cooperativism" is a movement that holds that digital platforms should be owned by, governed by, and should enrich the participating value creators (Scholz, 2017; Scholz & Schneider, 2017). As an intersectional workerist tactic and political approach, it extends earlier forms of cooperativism into the digital world. Platforms whose fixity currently enables a premium of predatory policies to de-contextualize and re-interpret user engagement could become elective "rules of the game," enacting computational processes necessary for particular projects that can be collectively re-negotiated or exited by users for whom they do not work. Platform cooperatives could help massively scaled groups affiliate based on agreements that allow consenting users to become an equally viable part of the network because of their participation. Collectivizing based on the corporate exploitation of social connection can generate a widespread awareness that, despite the limits inherent in communication, we can nevertheless hone and channel our signifying perfusion. The anarchic principle of free association emerges as far as it is only possible to hold tools of connectivity in common. Such a mode of engagement has the potential to foster collectives guided by common discontents, whatever they may be.

REFERENCES

Acker, C. J. (2002). *Creating the American junkie: Addiction research in the classic era of narcotic control.* Baltimore, MD: Johns Hopkins University Press.

Adams, R. A., Huys, Q. J. M., & Roiser, J. P. (2016). Computational Psychiatry: Towards a mathematically informed understanding of mental illness. *Journal of Neurology, Neurosurgery & Psychiatry*, 87(1), 53–63.

Alexander, B. K. (2008). *The globalisation of addiction: A study in poverty of the spirit.* Oxford, UK: Oxford University Press.

Alliez, É., Colebrook, C., Hallward, P., Thoburn, N., & Gilbert, J. (2010). Deleuzian politics? A roundtable discussion. *New Formations*, 68(68), 143–187.

Althusser, L. (2014). *On the reproduction of capitalism: Ideology and ideological state apparatuses.* London: Verso.

Anderson, M. S., Berger, J., Berger, M., Gray, L., Osborne, K., & Weider, A. (Producers), & Weider, A. (Director). (2012). Wecome to the machine [Documentary film]. USA: Loop Filmworks.

Arvidsson, A., & Colleoni, E. (2012). Value in informational capitalism and on the internet. *The Information Society*, 28(3), 135–150.

Barabási, A. L., & Bonabeau, E. (2003, May). Scale-free networks. *Scientific American*, 288(5), 60–69.

Barnes, S. J., & Pressey, A. D. (2014). Caught in the web? Addictive behavior in cyberspace and the role of goal-orientation. *Technological Forecasting and Social Change*, 86, 93–109.

Baron, M. L., Davis, J., Dow, T., Godfrey, W., Kilkenny, J., Lassiter, J., ... Smith, W. (Producers), & Proyas, A. (Director). (2004). I, robot [Motion picture]. USA: 20th Century Fox.

Bard, A., & Soderqvist, J. (2018). *Digital libido: Sex, power and violence in the network society.* Futurica Media.

Bateson, G. (2000). *Steps to an ecology of mind.* University of Chicago Press.

Berardi, F. (2009). *The soul at work: From alienation to autonomy.* Semiotext(e).

Bernardi, S., & Pallanti, S. (2009). Internet addiction: A descriptive clinical study focusing on comorbidities and dissociative symptoms. *Comprehensive Psychiatry*, 50(6), 510–516. https://doi.org/10.1016/j.comppsych.2008.11.011.

Black, D. W. (2013). *Behavioural addictions as a way to classify behaviours.* Los Angeles, CA: SAGE Publications Sage CA.

Block, J. J. (2008). Issues for DSM-V: Internet addiction. *American Journal of Psychiatry*, 165(3), 306–307.

Blodget, H. (2012, December 20). REVEALED: The full story of how Facebook IPO buyers got screwed. *Business Insider.* Retrieved from https://www.businessinsider.com/how-facebook-ipo-investors-got-screwed-2012-12.

Boltanski, L., & Chiapello, E. (2005). *The new spirit of capitalism.* Verso.

Boltanski, L., & Esquerre, A. (2016). The economic life of things. Commodities, collectibles, assets. *New Left Review*, 98, 31–54.

Bratton, B. H. (2015). *The stack: On software and sovereignty.* Boston, MA: MIT press.

Brown, W. (2006). American nightmare: Neoliberalism, neoconservatism, and de-democratization. *Political Theory*, 34(6), 690–714.

Brunetti, D., Chaffin, C., Davidson, J., De Luca, M., Rudin, S., Smythe, R., & Spacey, K. (Producers), & Fincher, D. (Director). (2010). The social network [Motion picture]. USA: Columbia Pictures.

Buchanan, I. (2008). *Deleuze and Guattari's' Anti-Oedipus: A reader's guide.* London, England: Continuum.

Burbach, R., Jeffries, F., & Robinson, W. I. (2001). *Globalization and postmodern politics: From Zapatistas to high-tech robber barons.* London, England: Pluto Press.

Caplan, S. E. (2005). A social skill account of problematic Internet use. *Journal of Communication*, 55(4), 721–736.

Christensen, J. B. (2015). *Addiction trajectories* (vii, 338 pp., illus., bibliogr.). (E. Raikhel & W. Garriott, Eds.). Durham, N.C.: Duke Univ. Press, 2013. £16.99 (paper). *Journal of the Royal Anthropological Institute*, 21(1), 231–232. https://doi.org/10.1111/1467-9655.12157_20.

Chun, W. H. K. (2011). *Programmed visions: Software and memory.* Cambridge, MA: MIT Press.

Chun, W. H. K. (2016). *Updating to remain the same: Habitual new media.* Cambridge, MA: MIT press.

Courtwright, D. T. (2010). The NIDA brain disease paradigm: History, resistance and spinoffs. *BioSocieties*, 5(1), 137–147.

Crary, J. (2013). *24/7: Late capitalism and the ends of sleep.* London, England: Verso.

Culp, A. (2019). A method to the madness: The revolutionary Marxist method of Deleuze and Guattari. *Stasis*, 7(1).

Daly, J., Gibson, D., & Hurd, G. A. (Producers), & Cameron, J. (Director). (1984). The terminator [Motion picture]. USA: Orion.

Davis, R. A. (2001). A cognitive-behavioral model of pathological Internet use. *Computers in Human Behavior*, 17(2), 187–195. https://doi.org/10.1016/S0747-5632(00)00041-8.

Davis, F. D., Riedl, R., vom Brocke, J., Léger, P.-M., & Randolph, A. B. (2019). *Information systems and neuroscience: NeuroIS retreat 2018.* https://doi.org/10.1007/978-3-030-01087-4.

Dean, J. (2010). *Blog theory: Feedback and capture in the circuits of drive.* Cambridge.

Dean, J. (2013). Complexity as capture—Neoliberalism and the loop of drive. *New Formations,* (80/81), 138–154.

Deleuze, G. (1986). *Cinema.* University of Minnesota.

Deleuze, G. (1990). *The logic of sense* (C. V. Boundas , Ed.; M. Lester & C. Stivale, Trans.). New York, NY: Columbia University Press. (Original work published 1969).

Deleuze, G. (1992). Postscript on the societies of control. *October, 59,* 3–7.

Deleuze, G. (1994). *Difference and repetition* (P. Patton, Trans.). New York, NY: Columbia University Press. (Original work published 1968).

Deleuze, G. (1995). Control and becoming. *Negotiations: 1972–1990* (pp. 169–176). Colombia University Press.

Deleuze, G. (1997). *Negotiations, 1972–90.* Columbia University Press.

Deleuze, G. (2004). *Desert islands and other texts, 1953–1974.* Semiotext(e); Distributed by MIT Press.

Deleuze, G., & Guattari, F. (1986). *Anti-Oedipus* (R. Hurley, M. Seem, & H. R. Lane, Trans.). Minneapolis: University of Minnesota Press. (Original work published 1972).

Deleuze, G., & Guattari, F. (1987). *A thousand plateaus* (B. Massumi, Trans.). Minneapolis: University of Minnesota Press. (Original work published 1980).

Deleuze, G., & Parnet, C. (2007). *Dialogues II* (Revised edition). Columbia University Press.

Dutton, W., Law, G., Bolsover, G., & Dutta, S. (2013). *The internet trust bubble: Global values, beliefs, and practices.* Davos: World Economic Forum.

Dyer-Witheford, N. (2015). *Cyber-proletariat: Global labour in the digital vortex.* Between the Lines; Pluto Press.

Elmer, G. (2017). Precorporation: Or what financialisation can tell us about the histories of the internet. *Internet Histories,* 1(1–2), 90–96. doi: 10.1080/24701475.2017.1308197.

Ernst, W. (2013). *Digital memory and the archive* (J. Parikka, Ed.). Minneapolis: University of Minnesota Press.

Firat, M. (2013). Multitasking or continuous partial attention: A critical bottleneck for digital natives. *Turkish Online Journal of Distance Education,* 14(1), 266–272.

Flick, C. (2016). Informed consent and the Facebook emotional manipulation study. *Research Ethics,* 12(1), 14–28.

Foti, A. (2017). *General theory of the precariat: Great recession, revolution, reaction.* Institute of Network Cultures.

Foucault, M. (1965). *Madness and civilization* (R. Howard, Trans.). New York, NY: Pantheon.

Foucault, M. (1988). *Technologies of the self: A seminar with Michel Foucault* (L. H., Martin, H., Gutman, & P. H., Hutton, Eds.). University of Massachusetts Press.

Foucault, M. (2007). *Security, territory, population: Lectures at the College de France, 1977–1978* (G. Burchell, Trans.). Basingstoke, England: Palgrave Macmillan.

Frischmann, B. M. (2012). *Infrastructure: The social value of shared resources.* Oxford University Press.

Frischmann, B., & Selinger, E. (2018). *Re-engineering humanity.* Cambridge, England: Cambridge University Press.

Fuchs, C. (2014). Digital prosumption labour on social media in the context of the capitalist regime of time. *Time & Society,* 23(1), 97–123.

Fuchs, C. (2019). *Rereading Marx in the age of digital capitalism.* Pluto Press.

Fuller, M. (Ed.). (2008). *Software studies: A lexicon.* MIT Press.

Gaebel, W., Zielasek, J., & Reed, G. M. (2017). Mental and behavioural disorders in the ICD-11: Concepts, methodologies, and current status. *Psychiatria Polska,* 51(2), 169–195. https://doi.org/10.12740/PP/69660.

Galloway, A. (2012). *The interface effect.* London, England: Polity.

Gerlitz, C., & Helmond, A. (2011, January). Hit, link, like and share: Organizing the social and the fabric of the web in a like economy. Paper presented at the DMI mini-conference, University of Amsterdam, the Netherlands. Retrieved from https://research.gold.ac.uk/7075/1/GerlitzHelmond-HitLinkLikeShare.pdf.

Gillespie, T. (2010). The politics of "platforms". *New Media & Society,* 12(3), 347–364.

Guattari, F. (1984). *Molecular revolution: Psychiatry and politics.* Penguin.

Guattari, F. (1995). *Chaosmosis: An ethico-aesthetic paradigm.* Indiana University Press.

Guattari, F. (1996). *Soft subversions* (S. Lotringer, Ed.). New York: Semiotext (e).

Guattari, F. (2008). *The three ecologies.* Continuum.

Guattari, F. (2011). *The machinic unconscious: Essays in schizoanalysis.* Semiotext(e); Distributed by the MIT Press.

Guattari, F. (2013). *Schizoanalytic cartographies* (p. 186). (A. Goffey, Trans.). London, England: Bloomsbury.

Guattari, F. (2015). *Psychoanalysis and transversality: Texts and interviews 1955-1971.* Semiotext(e).

Haider, A. (2018). *Mistaken identity: Race and class in the age of Trump.* Verso.

Han, B.-C., & DeMarco, A. (2017). *Topology of violence.* MIT Press.

Haraway, D. J. (1991). *Simians, cyborgs, and women: The reinvention of nature.* Routledge.

Hardt, M., & Negri, A. (1994). *Labor of Dionysus: A critique of the state-form.* University of Minnesota Press.

Hardt, M., & Negri, A. (2004). *Multitude: War and democracy in the age of Empire.* New York, NY: Penguin.

Hardt, M., & Negri, A. (2017). *Assembly.* Oxford University Press.

Harper, T., & Savat, D. (2016). *Media after Deleuze.* Bloomsbury Academic, an imprint of Bloomsbury Publishing Plc.

Harvey, D. (2018). *Marx, capital and the madness of economic reason.* Oxford University Press.

Harvey, D., & Marx, K. (2010). *A companion to Marx's Capital.* Verso.

Hern, A. (2018, January 24). Facebook should be 'regulated like cigarette industry', says tech CEO. *The Guardian.* https://www.theguardian.com/technology/2018/jan/24/facebook-regulated-cigarette-industry-salesforce-marc-benioff-social-media.

Hodges, D. C. (2000). *Class politics in the information age*. Champaign: University of Illinois Press.

Hui, Y., & Halpin, H. (2013). Collective individuation: The future of the social web. In G. Lovink, & M. Rasch (Eds.), *Unlike us reader: Social media monopolies and their alternatives* (pp. 103–116). Amsterdam, the Netherlands: Institute of Network Cultures.

Ippolita. (2015). *In the Facebook aquarium: The resistible rise of anarcho-capitalism* (P. Riemens & C. Landman, Trans.). Amsterdam, the Netherlands: Institute of Network Cultures.

Ippolita Collective, Lovink, G., & Rossiter, N. (2009). The digital given: 10 Web 2.0 theses. Fibreculture, 14. Retrieved from http://journal.fibreculture.org/issue14/issue14_ippolita_et_al_print.html.

Kardaras, N. (2017). *Glow kids: How screen addiction is hijacking our kids - and how to break the trance*. Reprint Edition (September 26, 2017). St. Martin's Griffin.

Kennedy, J. (2013). Rhetorics of sharing: Data, imagination and desire. In G. Lovink & M. Rasch (Eds.), *Unlike us reader: Social media monopolies and their alternatives* (pp. 127–136). Amsterdam, the Netherlands: Institute of Networked Culture.

Kirkpatrick, D. (2011). *The Facebook effect: The inside story of the company that is connecting the world*. New York, NY: Simon & Schuster.

Kleiner, D. (2010). *The telekommunist manifesto*. Institute of Network Cultures.

Klossowski, P., Smith, D. W., Morar, N., & Cisney, V. W. (2017). *Living Currency: Followed by Sade and Fourier*. http://search.ebscohost.com/login.aspx?direct=true&scope=site&db=nlebk&db=nlabk&AN=1717410.

Kordela, K. (2018). *Epistemontology in Spinoza-Marx-Freud-Lacan: The (bio)power of structure*. New York, NY: Routledge.

Kramer, A. D. I., Guillory, J. E., & Hancock, J. T. (2014). Experimental evidence of massive-scale emotional contagion through social networks. *Proceedings of the National Academy of Sciences*, 111(24), 8788–8790. https://doi.org/10.1073/pnas.1320040111.

Lacan, J. (2002). *The seminar of Jacques Lacan: Book XIV: The logic of phantasy 1966-67* (C. Gallagher, Trans.). New York, NY: Karnac.

Lacan, J. (2006). The direction of the treatment and the principles of its power. In B. Fink (Trans.), *Écrits* (pp. 489–542). New York, NY: W.W. Norton & Company. (Original work published 1966).

Lacan, J. (2007). *The seminar of Jacques Lacan: Book XVII. The other side of psychoanalysis: 1969-70* (J.-A. Miller, Ed.; R. Grigg, Trans.). London, England: W. W. Norton. (Original work published 1991).

LaRose, R., Lin, C. A., & Eastin, M. S. (2003). Unregulated Internet usage: Addiction, habit, or deficient self-regulation? *Media Psychology*, 5(3), 225–253.

Lazzarato, M. (2014). *Signs and machines: Capitalism and the production of subjectivity* (J. D. Jordan, Ed.). Los Angeles: Semiotext (e).

Levin, S. (2018, December 13). 'They don't care': Facebook factchecking in disarray as journalists push to cut ties. *The Guardian*. https://www.theguardian.com/technology/2018/dec/13/they-dont-care-facebook-fact-checking-in-disarray-as-journalists-push-to-cut-ties.

Levine, H. G. (1978). The discovery of addiction. Changing conceptions of habitual drunkenness in America. *Journal of Studies on Alcohol*, 39(1), 143–174.

Levy, N. (2013, April 11). Addiction is not a brain disease (and it matters). *Frontiers in Psychiatry*, 4(24). doi: 10.3389/fpsyt.2013.00024.

Loose, R. (2015). The hijacking of the symptom and the addictification of society. *Subjectivity*, 8(2), 165–179.

Lovink, G. (2011). *Networks without a cause: A critique of social media*. London, England: Polity.

Lovink, G. (2019). *Sad by design: On platform nihilism*. 1st Edition (June 15, 2019). Pluto Press.

Lovink, G., & Rasch, M. (Eds.). (2013). *Unlike us reader: Social media monopolies and their alternatives*. Amsterdam, the Netherlands: Institute of Network Cultures.

Lukács, G., & Livingstone, R. (2013). *History and class consciousness: Studies in Marxist dialects* (Nachdr.). MIT Press.

Malabou, C. (2012). *The new wounded: From neurosis to brain damage*. New York, NY: Fordham University Press.

Manjikian, M. (2016). *Threat talk: The comparative politics of Internet Addiction*. Routledge.

Marx, K. (1978). The German ideology: Part one. In R. C. Tucker (Ed.), *The Marx-Engels Reader* (2nd ed.). New York, NY: Norton. (Original work published 1932).

Marx, K. (1990). *Capital* (Vol. 1) (B. Fowkes, Ed.). London, England: Penguin Books. (Original work published 1867).

Marx, K. (1993). *Grundrisse: Foundations of the critique of political economy* (R. Draft & M. Nicolaus, Trans.). London, England: Penguin Books & New Left Review. (Original work published 1939–41).

Mazzucato, M. (2018). *The value of everything: Making and taking in the global economy*. Allen Lane, an imprint of Penguin Books.

McGowan, T. (2012). *The end of dissatisfaction? Jacques Lacan and the emerging society of enjoyment*. New York, NY: SUNY Press.

McLuhan, M. (1975). McLuhan's laws of the media. *Technology and culture*, 16(1), 74–78.

McNamee, R. (2017, November 11). How Facebook and Google threaten public health ⌐ and democracy. *The Guardian*. https://www.theguardian.com/commentisfree/2017/nov/11/facebook-google-public-health-democracy.

Mitropoulos, A. (2012). *Contract & contagion: From biopolitics to oikonomia*. Wivenhoe, England: Minor Compositions.

Montague, P. R., Dayan, P., & Sejnowski, T. J. (1996). A framework for mesencephalic dopamine systems based on predictive Hebbian learning. *Journal of Neuroscience*, 16(5), 1936–1947.

Morozov, E. (2015, Jan-Feb). *Socialize the data centres! New Left Review*, 91. Retrieved from https://newleftreview.org/issues/II91/articles/evgeny-morozov-socialize-the-data-centres.

Murphy, B. (2002). A critical history of the internet. In G. Elmer (Ed.), *Critical perspectives on the internet* (pp. 27–45). Boulder, CO: Rowman & Littlefield.

Negri, A. (2003). Constitutive time A and B. In M. Mandarini (Trans.), *Time for revolution* (pp. 83–108). London, England: Bloomsbury.

Novembre, G., Zanon, M., & Silani, G. (2014). Empathy for social exclusion involves the sensory-discriminative component of pain: A within-subject fMRI study. *Social Cognitive and Affective Neuroscience*, 10(2), 153–164. https://doi.org/10.1093/scan/nsu038.

Orford, J. (2001). *Excessive appetites: A psychological view of addictions.* Chichester, England: John Wiley & Sons.

Parker, I. (1999). Critical psychology: Critical links. *Annual Review of Critical Psychology*, 1(1), 3–18.

Parker, I. (2007). Psychoanalytic cyberspace, beyond psychology. *The Psychoanalytic Review*, 94(1), 63–82.

Pasquale, F. (2015). *The black box society.* Boston, MA: Harvard University Press.

Patelis, K. (2013). Political economy and monopoly abstractions: What social media demand. In G. Lovink & M. Rasch (Eds.), *Unlike us reader: Social media monopolies and their alternatives* (pp. 118–126). Amsterdam, the Netherlands: Institute of Network Cultures.

Phillips, L., & Rozworski, M. (2019). *The People's republic of Walmart: How the world's biggest corporations are laying the foundation for socialism.* Verso.

Potenza, M. N. (2014). Non-substance addictive behaviors in the context of DSM-5. *Addictive Behaviors*, 39(1), 1–2. https://doi.org/10.1016/j.addbeh.2013.09.004

Reinarman, C. (2005). Addiction as accomplishment: The discursive construction of disease. *Addiction Research & Theory*, 13, 307–320. doi: 10.1080/16066350500077728.

Rose, N. (2003). The neurochemical self and its anomalies. In R. V. Ericson & A. Doyle (Eds.), *Risk and morality* (pp. 407–437). Toronto, Canada: University of Toronto Press.

Rose, N. (2013). The human sciences in a biological age. *Theory, Culture & Society*, 30(1), 3–34. doi: 10.1177/0263276412456569.

Saikia, A. M., Das, J., Barman, P., & Bharali, M. D. (2019). Internet Addiction and its Relationships with Depression, Anxiety, and Stress in Urban Adolescents of Kamrup District, Assam. *Journal of Family & Community Medicine*, 26(2), 108–112. PubMed. https://doi.org/10.4103/jfcm.JFCM_93_18.

Sanders, R. (1987). The Pareto principle: its use and abuse. *Journal of Services Marketing*, 1(2), 37–40.

Schäfer, S., Sülflow, M., & Müller, P. (2017, April 3). The special taste of snack news: An application of niche theory to understand the appeal of Facebook as a news source. First Monday, 22(4). Retrieved from https://firstmonday.org/ojs/index.php/fm/article/view/7431 doi: 10.5210/fm.v22i4.7431.

Schneider, J. W. (1978). Deviant drinking as disease: Alcoholism as a social accomplishment. *Social Problems*, 25(4), 361–372.

Scholz, T. (2017). *Uberworked and underpaid: How workers are disrupting the digital economy.* Cambridge, England: Polity.

Scholz, T., & Schneider, N. (Eds.). (2017). *Ours to hack and own: The rise of platform cooperativism, a new vision for the future of work and a fairer internet.* New York, NY: OR Books.

Schultz, W. (1997). Dopamine neurons and their role in reward mechanisms. *Current Opinion in Neurobiology*, 7(2), 191–197.

Sedgwick, E. K. (1993). Epidemics of the will. *Tendencies* (pp. 130–142), Durham, NC: Duke University Press. doi: 10.1215/9780822381860-007.

Serres, M. (1995). *The natural contract* (E. MacArthur & W. Paulson, Trans.). Ann Arbor: University of Michigan Press. (Original work published 1990).

Sevignani, S. (2013). Facebook vs. diaspora: A critical study. In G. Lovink & M. Rasch (Eds.), *Unlike us reader: Social media monopolies and their alternatives* (pp. 323–337). Amsterdam, the Netherlands: Institute of Network Cultures.

Shepherd, T., & Landry, N. (2013). Technology design and power: Freedom and control in communication networks. *International Journal of Media & Cultural Politics*, 9(3), 259–275.

Simondon, G. (2014). *Sur la technique (1953–1983)*. Presses universitaires de France.

Snodgrass, J. G., Lacy, M. G., Dengah, H. F., II, Fagan, J., & Most, D. E. (2011). Magical flight and monstrous stress: Technologies of absorption and mental wellness in Azeroth. *Culture, Medicine, and Psychiatry*, 35(1), 26–62. doi: 10.1007/sll013-010-9197-4.

Soler, C. (2016). *Lacanian affects: The function of affect in Lacan's work* (B. Fink, Trans.). New York, NY: Routledge.

Solon, O. (2018, January 26). George Soros: Facebook and Google a menace to society. *The Guardian*. https://www.theguardian.com/business/2018/jan/25/george-soros-facebook-and-google-are-a-menace-to-society.

Srnicek, N., & Williams, A. (2016). *Inventing the future: Postcapitalism and a world without work* (Revised and updated edition). Verso.

Stalder, F. (2006). *Manuel Castells*. London, England: Polity.

Stiegler, B. (1998). Temps et individuations technique, psychique et collective dans l'oeuvre de Simondon [Technical, psychic, and collective time and individuation in the works of Simondon]. *Intellectica*, 26(1), 241–256.

Stiegler, B. (2005). Individuation et grammatisation: quand la technique fait sens ... [Individuation and grammatisation: When technique makes sense ...]. *Documentaliste-Sciences de l'Information*, 42(6), 354–360.

Stiegler, B. (2013). The most precious good in the era of social technologies. *Unlike Us Reader. Social Media Monopolies and Their Alternatives* (pp. 16–30). Amsterdam: Institute of Network Cultures.

Terranova, T. (2014). Red Stack Attack!. In Robin Mackay & Armen Avanessian (Eds.), *#Accelerate: The accelerationist reader*. Falmouth: Urbanomic.

Thoburn, N. (2003). *Deleuze, Marx and politics*. Routledge.

Thompson, D. (2012, February 2). The profit network: Facebook and its 835 million-man workforce. *The Atlantic*. Retrieved from https://www.theatlantic.com/business/archive/2012/02/the-profit-network-facebook-and-its-835-million-man-workforce/252473/.

Trigo, J. M., Martin-García, E., Berrendero, F., Robledo, P., & Maldonado, R. (2010). The endogenous opioid system: A common substrate in drug addiction. *Drug and Alcohol Dependence*, 108(3), 183–194.

Tuck, E. (2010). Breaking up with Deleuze: desire and valuing the irreconcilable. *International Journal of Qualitative Studies in Education*, 23(5), 635–650. doi: 10.1080/09518398.2010.500633.

Turkle, S. (2005). *The second self: Computers and the human spirit*. Cambridge, MA: MIT Press.

Turkle, S. (2015). *Reclaiming conversation: The power of talk in a digital age*. Penguin Press.

Vaidhyanathan, S. (2012). *The Googlization of everything (and why we should worry)*. Berkeley: University of California Press.

Valverde, M. (1998). *Diseases of the will: Alcohol and the dilemmas of freedom* (p. 197). Cambridge, England: Cambridge University Press.

Varakin, D. A., Levin, D. T., & Fidler, R. (2004). Unseen and unaware: Implications of recent research on failures of visual awareness for human-computer interface design. *Human-Computer Interaction*, 19(4), 389–422.

Volkow, N. D., & O'Brien, C. P. (2007). Issues for DSM-V: Should obesity be included as a brain disorder? *American Journal of Psychiatry*, 164(5), 708–710. doi: 10.1176/ajp.2007.164.5.708.

Vrecko, S. (2010). Birth of a brain disease: Science, the state and addiction neuropolitics. *History of the Human Sciences*, 23(4), 52–67. doi: 10.1177/0952695110371598.

Wark, M. (2004). *A hacker manifesto*. Cambridge, MA: Harvard University Press.

Wark, M. (2006). Information wants to be free (but is everywhere in chains). *Cultural Studies*, 20(2-3), 165–183.

Wark, M. (2015). *Molecular red: Theory for the anthropocene*. London, England: Verso Books.

Weber, S., & Wong, R. Y. (2017, February 6). The new world of data: Four provocations on the internet of things. First Monday, 22(2). Retrieved from https://firstmonday.org/ojs/index.php/fm/article/view/6936.

Weinberg, D. (2013). Post-humanism, addiction and the loss of self-control: Reflections on the missing core in addiction science. *International Journal of Drug Policy*, 24(3), 173–181.

Wynn, N. [ContraPoints]. (2019, January 16). *Are Traps Gay?* [Video]. YouTube. https://www.youtube.com/watch?v=PbBzhqJK3bg.

Young, K. S., & Rogers, R. C. (1998). The relationship between depression and Internet addiction. *Cyberpsychology & Behavior*, 1(1), 25–28.

Žižek, S. (1997). *The plague of fantasies*. London, England: Verso.

Žižek, S. (1999). *The ticklish subject: The absent centre of political ontology*. London, England: Verso.

Zupančič, A. (2017). *What is sex?* Boston, MA: MIT Press.

Zwick, D., & Dholakia, N. (2006). The epistemic consumption object and post-social consumption: Expanding consumer object theory in consumer research. *Consumption, Markets and Culture*, 9(1), 17–43.

INDEX

Printed in the United States
by Baker & Taylor Publisher Services

Printed in the United States
by Baker & Taylor Publisher Services